Experiencing Choral Music

PROFICIENT

SIGHT-SINGING

Developed by

HAL•LEONARD® CORPORATION

Mc Graw Hill **Glencoe**

New York, New York   Columbus, Ohio   Chicago, Illinois

The McGraw·Hill Companies

Printed in the United States of America.

Send all inquiries to:
Glencoe/McGraw-Hill
8787 Orion Place,
Columbus,OH 43240-4027

ISBN 0-07-861128-8

12 13   MAL   15 14 13 12

Credits

AUTHORS

Emily Crocker
Vice President of Choral Publications
Hal Leonard Corporation, Milwaukee, Wisconsin
Founder and Artistic Director, Milwaukee Children's Choir

Audrey Snyder
Composer
Eugene, Oregon

EDITORIAL

Linda Rann
Senior Editor
Hal Leonard Corporation, Milwaukee, Wisconsin

Stacey Nordmeyer
Choral Editor
Hal Leonard Corporation, Milwaukee, Wisconsin

Table of Contents

CHAPTER 1

Rhythm – The Beat, Quarter Note and Quarter Rest 1

Terms and Symbols – Barline and Measure 2

Rhythm – Time Signature • 4/4 Meter 2

Pitch – The Staff, Treble Clef and Bass Clef, The Grand Staff 3

Pitch – The Scale, Key 4

Rhythm – Half Note and Half Rest 5

Rhythm – Time Signature • 4/4 Meter and Common Time 6

Practice – Pitch and Rhythm • C Major 7

Rhythm – Dotted Half Note 8

Rhythm – Whole Note and Whole Rest 8

Practice – Pitch and Rhythm • C Major 9

Sight-Sing – *The Mountains* 10

Evaluation 12

CHAPTER 2

Pitch – The C Major Scale 13

Rhythm – Time Signature • 3/4 Meter 14

Pitch – Ledger Lines 15

Sight-Sing – *To Make A Prairie* 16

Pitch – The A Minor Scale 18

Practice – Pitch and Rhythm • A Minor in 3/4 and 4/4 Meter 19

Sight-Sing – *Sing Heigh Ho* 20

Evaluation 22

CHAPTER 3

Rhythm – Eighth Notes and Eighth Rests 23

Rhythm – Grouping Eighth Notes 24

Terms and Symbols – Double Barline, Repeat Sign 25

Pitch – The C Major Tonic Chord 26

Practice – Pitch and Rhythm • C Major in 4/4 Meter 27

Sight-Sing – *It's A Beautiful Day* 28

Pitch – Altered Pitches 30

Sight-Sing – *The House On The Hill* 32

Pitch – The C Major Tonic and Dominant Chords 34

Practice – Pitch and Rhythm • C Major Tonic and
Dominant Chords 35

Pitch – The A Minor Tonic and Dominant Chords 36

Pitch – More About Minor 37

Practice – Pitch and Rhythm • A Minor Tonic and
Dominant Chords 39

Sight-Sing – *Come And Be Merry* 40

Rhythm – Tied Notes 42

Evaluation 43

CHAPTER 4

Pitch – The F Major Scale 45

Pitch – The F Major Tonic and Dominant Chords 46

Sight-Sing – *Green Grows The Willow* 47

Rhythm – Reviewing Tied Notes 50

Rhythm – Dotted Half and Dotted Quarter Notes 51

Terms and Symbols – Dynamics 52

Sight-Sing – *Match Cats Road Trip* 52

Practice – Pitch and Rhythm • Dotted Notes in F Major 54

Sight-Sing – *Proverb* 55

Pitch – The D Minor Scale 56

Pitch – The D Minor Tonic and Dominant Chords 57

Sight-Sing – *My Peace* 58

Evaluation 61

CHAPTER 5

Rhythm – Sixteenth Notes 62

Rhythm – Sixteenth and Eighth Note Combinations 63

Rhythm – More Sixteenth and Eighth Note Combinations 64

Sight-Sing – *Restaurante Mexicano* 65

Rhythm – Time Signature • 2/4 Meter 66

Practice – Pitch and Rhythm • D Minor in 2/4 Meter 67

Sight-Sing – *Jubilate (Sing Joyfully)* 68

Pitch – The G Major Scale 71

Pitch – The G Major Tonic, Dominant and Subdominant Chords . . .72

Practice – Pitch and Rhythm • G Major Tonic, Dominant and
Subdominant Chords 73

Sight-Sing – *Morning* 74

Rhythm – Dotted Eighth and Sixteenth Note Combinations 76

Practice – Pitch and Rhythm •
Dotted Eighth and Sixteenth Notes in G Major 77

Pitch – The E Minor Scale 78

Pitch – The E Minor Tonic, Dominant and Subdominant Chords . . .79

Practice – Pitch and Rhythm • E Minor Tonic, Dominant and
Subdominant Chords 80

Sight-Sing – *Sail On, Clipper Ship* 81

Evaluation 84

CHAPTER 6

Terms and Symbols – Accent, Syncopation .85

Practice – Pitch and Rhythm • Syncopation in E Minor 86

Sight-Sing – *Blessed Song Of Peace* 87

Pitch – The Key of B♭ Major 90

Pitch – The B♭ Major Tonic, Dominant and Subdominant Chords . . .91

Practice – Pitch and Rhythm • B♭ Major Tonic, Dominant and
Subdominant Chords 92

Pitch – The B♭ Major Diatonic Chords 93

Sight-Sing – *Deo Gratias* 94

Pitch – The Key of G Minor 97

Pitch – The G Minor Tonic, Dominant and Subdominant Chords . . .98

Practice – Pitch and Rhythm • G Minor Tonic, Dominant and
Subdominant Chords 99

Sight-Sing – *Let The Bullgine Run* 100

Pitch – The Key of D Major 104

Pitch – The D Major Diatonic Chords 105

Practice – Pitch and Rhythm • D Major Diatonic Chords 106

Rhythm – Mixed Meter 107

Sight-Sing – *Match Cats Bebop* 108

Sight-Sing – *Brothers And Sisters* 109

Evaluation 112

CHAPTER 7

Rhythm – Simple Meter and Compound Meter 113

Rhythm – Time Signature • 6/8 Meter 114

Pitch – The Key of E♭ Major 115

Practice – Pitch and Rhythm • E♭ Major Tonic, Dominant and
Subdominant Chords 116

Rhythm – Time Signature • 6/8 and 9/8 Meter 117

Rhythm – Time Signature • 12/8 Meter 118

Practice – Pitch and Rhythm • E♭ Major in 12/8 Meter 119

Sight-Sing – *Summer Day* 120

Pitch – The Key of C Minor 122

Practice – Pitch and Rhythm • C Minor Tonic, Dominant and
Subdominant Chords 123

Sight-Sing – *Snowboarders* 124

Rhythm – Division of the Beat 127

Rhythm – More About Mixed Meter 128

Practice – Rhythm • Mixed Meter Combinations 129

Sight-Sing – *Two English Languages* 130

Rhythm – Mixed Meter in the Time Signature 132

Practice – Pitch and Rhythm • C Minor in Mixed Meter 133

Sight-Sing – *Roll On, River* 134

Evaluation 136

CHAPTER 8

Pitch – The Key of A Major 138

Practice – Pitch and Rhythm • Key of A Major 139

Pitch – The Key of F♯ Minor 140

Practice – Pitch and Rhythm • Key of F♯ Minor 141

Sight-Sing – *Irish Blessing* 142

Rhythm – More Simple Meters 146

Rhythm – Time Signature • 2/2 Meter and Cut Time 147

Sight-Sing – *Time* 148

Evaluation 151

CHAPTER 9

Pitch – The Circle of Fifths 152

Practice – Pitch and Rhythm • Key of A♭ Major 153

Practice – Pitch and Rhythm • Key of F Minor 154

Practice – Pitch and Rhythm • Key of E Major 155

Practice – Pitch and Rhythm • Key of C♯ Minor 156

Pitch – Modes and Modal Scales 157

Practice – Pitch and Rhythm • The D Dorian and F Lydian Scales . . .158

Practice – Pitch • The D Mixolydian Scale .159

Sight-Sing – *This Festive Night* 159

Evaluation 162

CHAPTER 10

Rhythm – Borrowed Division • Triplets and Duplets 164

Rhythm – More About Triplets and Duplets 165

Rhythm – More About Mixed Meter 166

Practice – Pitch and Rhythm • Mixed Meter 167

Sight-Sing – *Jubilate Deo* 168

Pitch – The Blues Scale 170

Rhythm – Swing Rhythms 171

Sight-Sing – *Singin' The Blues* 172

Pitch – Intervals, Consonant and Dissonant Intervals 175

Sight-Sing – *Prayer* 176

Evaluation 178

Appendix 179

TO THE STUDENT

Welcome to choir!

By singing in the choir, you have chosen to be a part of an exciting and rewarding adventure. The benefits of being in choir are many. Basically, singing is fun. It provides an expressive way of sharing your feelings and emotions. Through choir, you will have friends that share a common interest with you. You will experience the joy of making beautiful music together. Choir provides an opportunity to develop interpersonal skills. It takes teamwork and cooperation to sing together, and you must learn how to work with others. As you critique your individual and group performances, you can improve your ability to analyze and communicate your thoughts clearly.

Even if you do not pursue a music career, music can be an important part of your life. There are many avocational opportunities in music. **Avocational** means *not related to a job or career.* Singing as a hobby can provide you with personal enjoyment, enrich your life, and teach you life skills. Singing is something you can do for the rest of your life.

In this course, you will be presented with the basic skills of music notation and sight-singing. You will learn new concepts through exercises, combinable lines, speech choruses and original sight-singing practice songs. Guidelines for becoming a successful choir member include:

- Come to class prepared to learn.
- Respect the efforts of others.
- Work daily to improve your sight-singing skills.
- Sing expressively at all times.
- Have fun singing.

This book was written to provide you with a meaningful choral experience. Take advantage of the knowledge and opportunities offered here. Your exciting adventure of experiencing choral music is about to begin!

CHAPTER 1

Rhythm

◆ The Beat

Just as the heart beats with an even pulse, the **beat** is *the steady pulse of all music.*

◆ Quarter Note and Quarter Rest

Composers assign music notes and rests to represent the beat. In this case, a **quarter note** is *a note that represents one beat of sound* and a **quarter rest** is *a rest that represents one beat of silence.*

Quarter Note   Quarter Rest

◆ Practice

Tempo is *the speed at which the beat moves.* At a slow tempo, clap, tap or chant the following exercises to practice reading quarter notes and quarter rests. Then, clap, tap or chant the exercises at a faster tempo. Always keep the beat steady.

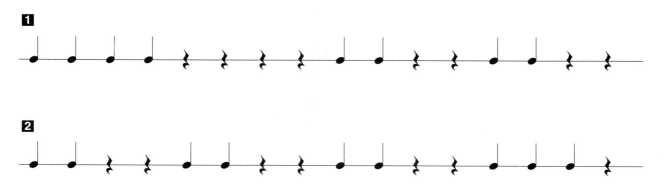

Terms and Symbols

◆ Barline and Measure

In music, a **barline** is *a vertical line that groups notes and rests together.* A **measure** is *the space between two barlines.*

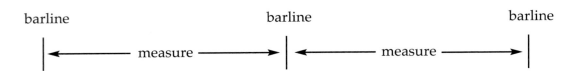

Any number of beats can be grouped in a measure. In the exercise below, there are four beats per measure. Clap, tap or chant the rhythm, keeping the beat steady.

Rhythm

◆ Time Signature • $\frac{4}{4}$ Meter

Meter is *a way of organizing rhythm.* A **time signature** (sometimes called a meter signature) is *the set of numbers at the beginning of a piece of music.*

$\frac{4}{4}$ **meter** is *a time signature in which there are four beats per measure and the quarter note receives the beat.*

4 The top number indicates the number of beats per measure.
4 The bottom number indicates the kind of note that receives the beat.

Clap, tap or chant the following exercise to practice reading rhythmic patterns in four.

Pitch

◆ The Staff

A **staff** is *a series of five horizontal lines and four spaces on which notes are written.* Notes are placed on a staff to indicate **pitch**, or *how high or low each note sounds.* A staff is like a ladder. Notes placed higher on the staff sound higher than notes placed lower on the staff.

higher pitch   lower pitch

Staff

◆ Treble Clef and Bass Clef

A **clef** is *the symbol at the beginning of a staff that indicates which lines and spaces represent which notes.* A **treble clef** is *a clef that generally indicates notes that sound higher than middle C.* A **bass clef** is *a clef that generally indicates notes that sound lower than middle C.*

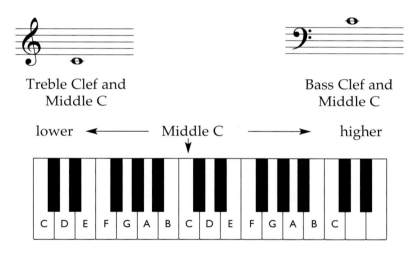

Treble Clef and
Middle C

Bass Clef and
Middle C

lower ← —— Middle C —— → higher

◆ The Grand Staff

A **grand staff** is *a staff that is created when two staves are joined together.* Again, the higher a note is placed on the staff, the higher its pitch. The lower a note is placed on the staff, the lower its pitch.

Middle C

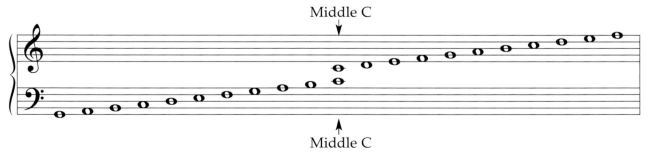

Middle C

Pitch

◆ The Scale

A **scale** is *a group of notes that are sung or played in succession and are based on a particular home tone, or keynote.* Here are two ways to visualize a scale.

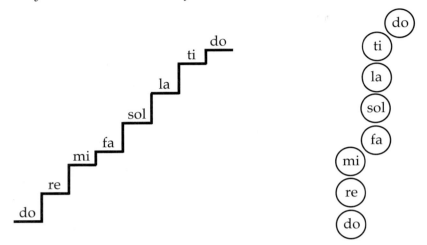

◆ Key

In a scale, the **key** is *determined by its home tone, or keynote.* For example, in the key of C major, C is the home tone. Sing the scale below.

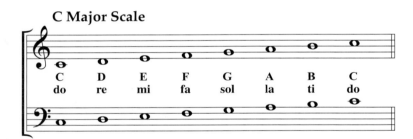

◆ Practice

Adjusting to fit your vocal range, read and echo the following exercises to practice singing notes from the C major scale.

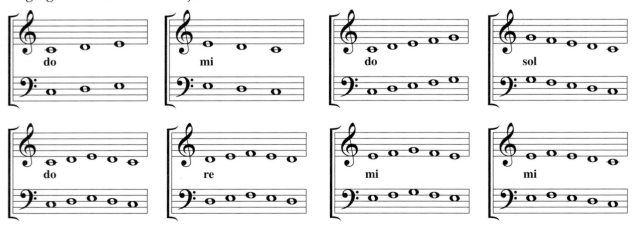

Rhythm

The **beat** is *the steady pulse of all music.* **Rhythm** is *the combination of long and short notes and rests.* These may move with the beat, faster than the beat or slower than the beat.

◆ Half Note and Half Rest

A **half note** is *a note that represents two beats of sound when the quarter note receives the beat.* A **half rest** is *a rest that represents two beats of silence when the quarter note receives the beat.*

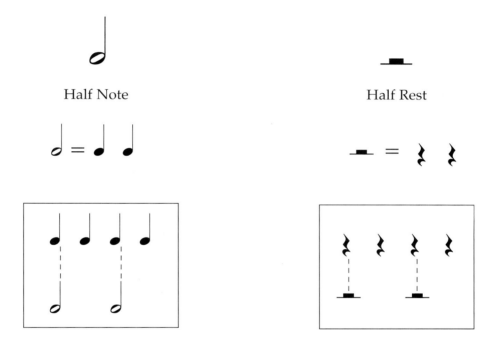

Half Note   Half Rest

◆ Practice

Clap, tap or chant the following exercises to practice reading half notes and half rests.

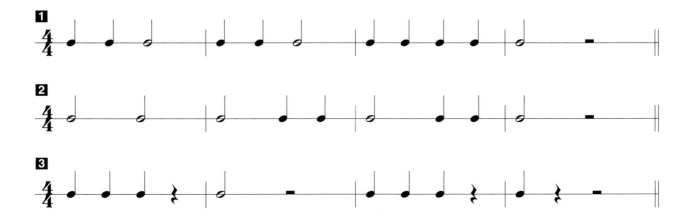

Rhythm

◆ Time Signature • $\frac{4}{4}$ Meter

$\frac{4}{4}$ **meter** is *a time signature in which there are four beats per measure and the quarter note receives the beat.*

4 = four beats per measure

4 = the quarter note receives the beat

Study and practice the conducting pattern to the right.

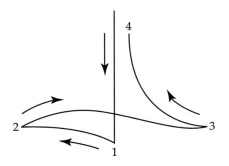

◆ Practice

Chant the rhythms in the following exercises as you conduct.

1

2

3

4

5

◆ Common Time • **C**

Common time, or common meter, is *another name for $\frac{4}{4}$ meter.* Clap, tap or chant the following exercise to practice reading rhythmic patterns in common time.

6

Practice

◆ Pitch and Rhythm • C Major

Now read pitch and rhythm together. Using notes from the C major scale below as a guide, sight-sing the following exercises by first clapping or chanting the rhythm. Then, selecting exercises to fit your vocal range, speak the pitch names using **solfège syllables** (*do, re, mi*). Finally, sing each exercise using solfège syllables. After singing each exercise separately, combine them in two, three or more parts.

◆ Challenge

Conduct in four while you sing.

Rhythm

◆ Dotted Half Note

A **dotted half note** is *a note that represents three beats of sound when the quarter note receives the beat.* Three beats of rests are represented by ▬ 𝄽 or 𝄽 ▬ .

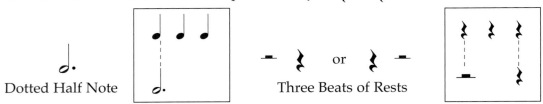

Dotted Half Note

Three Beats of Rests

◆ Practice

Clap, tap or chant the following exercises to practice reading dotted half notes.

◆ Whole Note and Whole Rest

A **whole note** is *a note that represents four beats of sound when the quarter note receives the beat.* A **whole rest** is *a rest that represents four beats of silence when the quarter note receives the beat.* In $\frac{4}{4}$ meter, a whole note represents one full measure of sound, and a whole rest represents one full measure of silence.

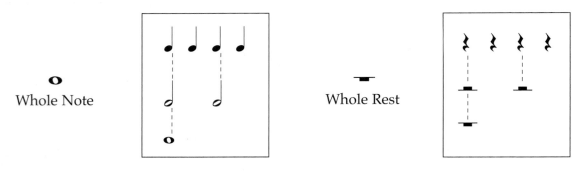

Whole Note

Whole Rest

◆ Practice

Clap, tap or chant the following exercises to practice reading whole notes and whole rests.

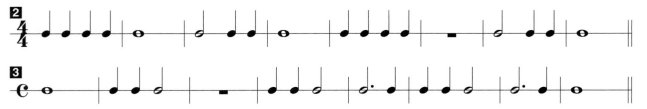

Practice

◆ Pitch and Rhythm • C Major

Using the notes from the C major scale below as a guide and selecting exercises to fit your vocal range, sight-sing the following exercises separately or in any combination.

◆ Challenge

Conduct in four while you sing.

The Mountains

Words and Music by
AUDREY SNYDER

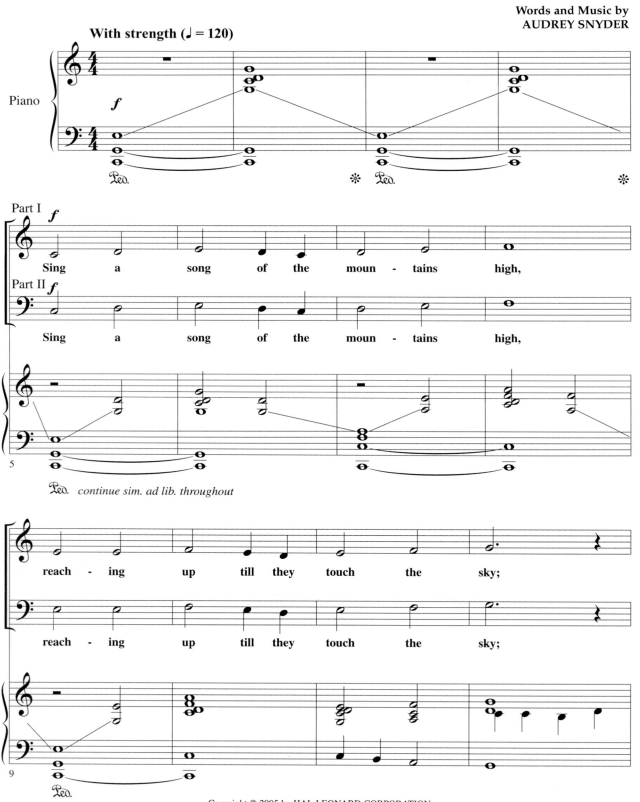

Evaluation

Demonstrate what you have learned in Chapter One by completing the following:

◆ Name the first five notes of the C major scale. Sing them using solfège syllables.

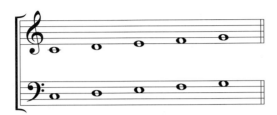

◆ **4** What does the top number mean in this time signature?

4 What does the bottom number mean?

◆ Name these kinds of notes and rests:

◆ **Mental Musical Math**
In $\frac{4}{4}$ meter:
1. One half note equals the same amount of time as how many quarter notes?
2. One dotted half note equals the same amount of time as how many quarter notes?

◆ Sight-sing the following exercises.

Pitch

◆ The C Major Scale

A **scale** is *a group of notes that are sung or played in succession and are based on a particular home tone, or keynote.*

Play a scale on the piano starting on C and ending on C, using only the white notes and without skipping any notes.

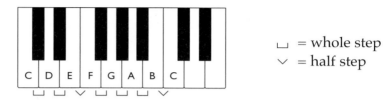

⊔ = whole step
∨ = half step

These notes form a pattern of whole steps and half steps. A **half step** is *the smallest distance between two notes.* A **whole step** is *the combination of two half steps side by side.*

The **major scale** is *a scale that has* do *as its home tone, or keynote.* It is made up of a specific arrangement of whole steps and half steps in the following order:

W + W + H + W + W + W + H

Sing the C major scale using solfège syllables. Where do the whole steps occur? Where do the half steps occur?

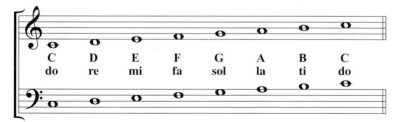

◆ Practice

Sight-sing the following exercises separately or in any combination.

Rhythm

◆ Time Signature • $\frac{3}{4}$ Meter

$\frac{3}{4}$ **meter** is *a time signature in which there are three beats per measure and the quarter note receives the beat*. A whole rest ▬ in $\frac{3}{4}$ meter represents one measure of silence.

4 = four beats per measure
4 = the quarter note receives the beat

3 = three beats per measure
4 = the quarter note receives the beat

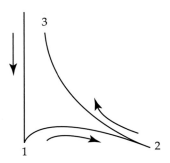

Study and practice the conducting pattern to the right.

◆ Practice

Chant the rhythms in the following exercises as you conduct.

Sight-sing the following exercises separately or in any combination.

Pitch

◆ Ledger Lines

Middle C can be written on its own short line in either treble or bass clef. Other notes can be written that way as well. These notes are written with **ledger lines**, or *short lines that are used to represent a note above or below the staff.*

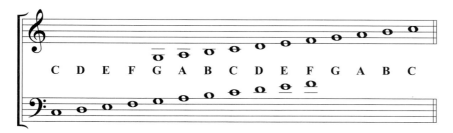

◆ Practice

Sight-sing the following exercises, separately or in any combination, that use notes with ledger lines.

◆ Challenge

Conduct in three while you sing.

To Make A Prairie

Poem by
EMILY DICKINSON (1830-1886)

Music by
EMILY CROCKER

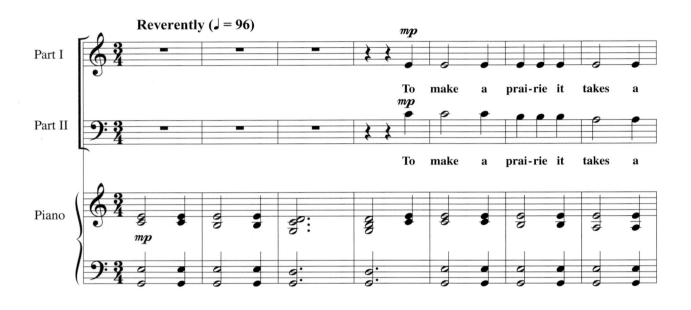

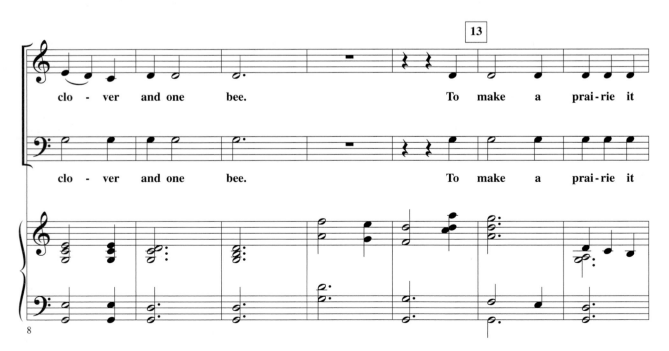

takes one clo - ver and a bee. And rev - er -

takes one clo - ver and a bee. And rev - er -

15

27

y, rev - er - y. The rev - er - y a -

y, rev - er - y. The rev - er - y a -

22

lone will do, If bees are few.

lone will do, If bees are few.

rit.

29

Pitch

◆ The A Minor Scale

The major scale is a specific arrangement of whole steps and half steps:

W + W + H + W + W + W + H

The C major scale is a major scale that starts and ends on C. The half steps occur between E and F *(mi and fa)* and B and C *(ti and do).*

Play a scale on the piano starting on A and ending on A, using only the white notes and without skipping any notes. Notice how different it sounds from a major scale.

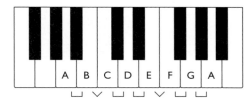

⊔ = whole step
∨ = half step

The **minor scale** is *a scale that has* la *as its home tone, or keynote.* It is made up of a specific arrangement of whole steps and half steps in the following order:

W + H + W + W + H + W + W

Sing the A minor scale using solfège syllables. Where do the whole steps occur? Where do the half steps occur?

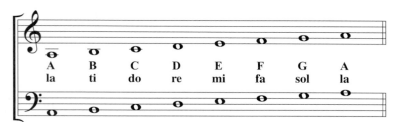

The A minor scale is called the relative minor of the C major scale since both scales have the same half steps (E and F, *mi* and *fa*; B and C, *ti* and *do*).

◆ Practice

Adjusting to fit your vocal range, read and echo the following exercises to practice singing notes from the A minor scale.

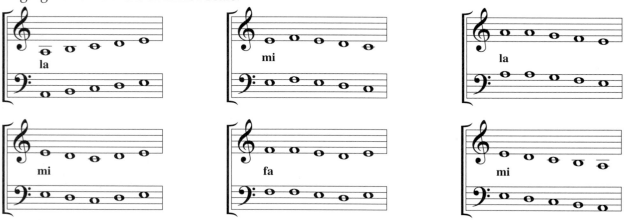

Practice

◆ Pitch and Rhythm • A Minor in $\frac{3}{4}$ and $\frac{4}{4}$ Meter

Using the A minor patterns below as a guide, sight-sing the following sets of exercises separately or in any combination.

Sing Heigh Ho

Words and Music by
EMILY CROCKER

Evaluation

Demonstrate what you have learned in Chapter Two by completing the following:

◆ Name the notes in the C major and A minor scales. Sing them using solfège syllables. Where are the half steps in each scale?

C Major Scale

A Minor Scale

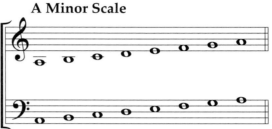
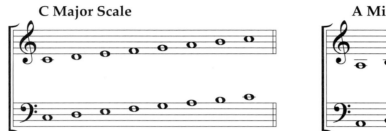

◆ Sight-sing the following melodies.

4 x 4

do

Three Of A Kind

la

◆ **Be A Composer**
Copy the rhythm below on a sheet of paper. Choose pitches from the C major scale for each note, then transfer them to a music staff. (You may want to start and end your melody on *do* or C.) Sing your melody using solfège syllables. Play your melody on a keyboard or create words for your melody.

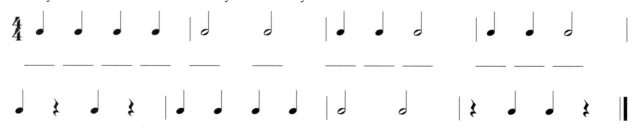

CHAPTER 3

Rhythm

◆ Eighth Notes and Eighth Rests

The **beat** is *the steady pulse of all music.* **Rhythm** is *the combination of long and short notes and rests.*

An **eighth note** is *a note that represents half a beat of sound when the quarter note receives the beat.* An **eighth rest** is *a rest that represents half a beat of silence when the quarter note receives the beat.*

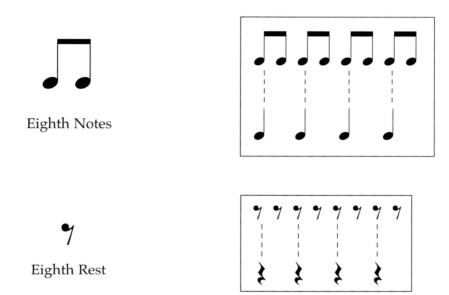

Eighth Notes

Eighth Rest

◆ Practice

Clap, tap or chant while conducting the following exercises to practice reading eighth notes.

Rhythm

◆ Grouping Eighth Notes

Eighth notes can be beamed together in groups, or they can be separated into single notes.

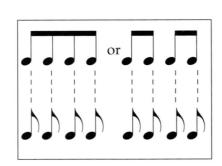

Two eighth notes equal the same length of time as one quarter note.

Two eighth rests equal the same length of time as one quarter rest.

◆ Practice

Clap, tap or chant the following exercises to practice reading eighth notes and eighth rests.

Terms and Symbols

◆ Double Barline ‖

A **double barline** is *a set of two barlines that indicate the end of a piece or section of music.*
The end of a piece of music may also be labeled "fine" *(FEE-nay).*

◆ Practice

Sight-sing the following exercise.

◆ Repeat Sign :‖

A **repeat sign** is *a symbol that indicates that a section of music should be repeated.*

◆ Practice

Sight-sing the following exercises, observing the repeat signs.

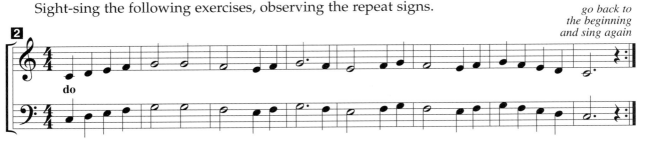

Pitch

◆ The C Major Tonic Chord

A **chord** is *the combination of three or more notes played or sung at the same time.* The **tonic chord** is *a chord built on the home tone, or keynote, of a scale.*

In a major scale, the tonic chord uses the notes *do, mi* and *sol*. This chord may be called the **I** ("one") chord, since it is based on the first note of the scale, or *do*.

C Major Tonic Chord

I — C do — E mi — G sol — C do

◆ Practice

An **interval** is *the distance between two notes.* Read and echo the following exercises to practice singing intervals found in the C major tonic chord.

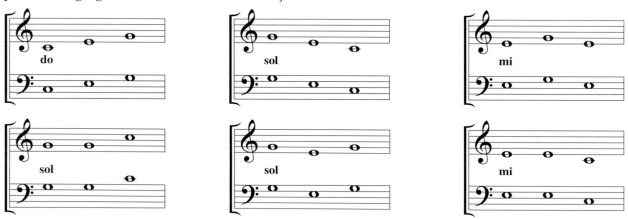

do

sol

mi

sol

sol

mi

Sight-sing the following exercises that use pitches found in the C major tonic chord.

1
do

2
do

3
do

Practice

◆ Pitch and Rhythm • C Major in $\frac{4}{4}$ Meter

Using the C major patterns below as a guide, sight-sing the following exercises by first clapping or chanting the rhythms. Then, selecting exercises to fit your vocal range, speak the pitch names using solfège syllables. Finally, sing each example using solfège syllables. After singing each exercise separately, combine them in two, three or more parts.

◆ Challenge

Conduct in four while you sing.

It's A Beautiful Day

Words and Music by
AUDREY SNYDER

Part I

It's a beau-ti-ful day, things are go-in' my way.

Part II

It's a beau-ti-ful day, things are go-in' my way.

Yes, it's a beau-ti-ful day, and things are go-in' my way.

Yes, it's a beau-ti-ful day, and things are go-in' my way.

Pitch

◆ Altered Pitches

Sometimes, altered pitches are used in music. An **accidental** (another name for an altered pitch) is *any sharp, flat or natural that is not included in the key signature of a piece of music.* For example, in the key of C major, D♯ would be an altered pitch, or accidental.

A sharp raises the
pitch one half step.

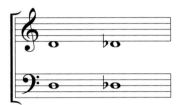

A flat lowers the
pitch one half step.

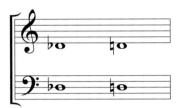

A natural cancels a
previous sharp or flat.

◆ Chromatic Scale

The **chromatic scale** is *a scale that consists of all half steps and uses all 12 pitches in an octave.*

◆ Practice

Sight-sing the following exercises in the key of C major that use altered pitches.

Di and Ra

Sharped *do* becomes *di*. Flatted *re* becomes *ra*. Notice that *di* and *ra* are the same pitch.

†*An altered pitch or accidental continues through the measure unless cancelled.*

The natural cancels the previous sharp.

Ri and Ma

Sharped *re* becomes *ri*. Flatted *mi* becomes *ma*. Notice that *ri* and *ma* are the same pitch.

Fi and Se

Sharped *fa* becomes *fi*. Flatted *sol* becomes *se*. Notice that *fi* and *se* are the same pitch.

Si and Le

Sharped *sol* becomes *si*. Flatted *la* becomes *le*. Notice that *si* and *le* are the same pitch.

Li and Te

Sharped *la* becomes *li*. Flatted *ti* becomes *te*. Notice that *li* and *te* are the same pitch.

The House On The Hill

Words and Music by
AUDREY SNYDER

Pitch

◆ The C Major Tonic and Dominant Chords

A **chord** is *the combination of three or more notes played or sung at the same time.* The **tonic chord** is *a chord built on the home tone, or keynote, of a scale.* In a major scale, this chord uses the notes *do, mi* and *sol* and is sometimes called the **I** ("one") chord, since it is based on the first note of the scale, or *do.*

Chords can be built on any note of the scale. The **dominant chord** is *a chord built on the fifth note of a scale.* In a major scale, this chord uses the notes *sol, ti* and *re* and is sometimes called the **V** ("five") chord, since it is based on the fifth note of the scale, or *sol.*

C Major Tonic Chord

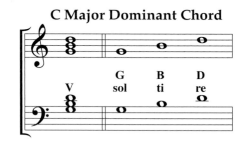

C Major Dominant Chord

◆ Practice

Read and echo the following exercises to practice singing patterns found in the C major tonic and dominant chords.

Sight-sing the following exercise that uses pitches found in the C major tonic and dominant chords.

Practice

◆ Pitch and Rhythm • C Major Tonic and Dominant Chords

Using the C major patterns below as a guide, sight-sing the following exercises separately or in any combination.

Pitch

◆ The A Minor Tonic and Dominant Chords

A **chord** is *the combination of three or more notes played or sung at the same time.* The **tonic chord** is *a chord built on the home tone, or keynote, of a scale.* In a minor scale, this chord uses the notes *la, do* and *mi* and is sometimes called the **i** ("one") chord, since it is based on the first note of the scale, or *la.*

The **dominant chord** is *a chord built on the fifth note of a scale.* In a minor scale, this chord uses the notes *mi, sol* and *ti* and is sometimes called the **v** ("five") chord, since it is based on the fifth note of the scale, or *mi.*

◆ Practice

Read and echo the following exercises to practice singing patterns found in the A minor tonic and dominant chords.

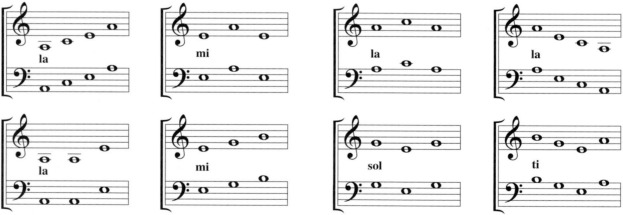

◆ Practice

Sight-sing the following exercise that uses pitches found in the A minor tonic and dominant chords.

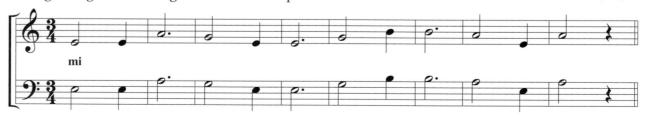

Pitch

◆ More About Minor

A **minor scale** is *a scale that has* la *as its home tone, or keynote*. It is made up of a specific arrangement of whole steps and half steps in the following order: W + H + W + W + H + W + W.

Sometimes, altered pitches are used in minor keys. A **sharp** (♯) is *a symbol that raises the pitch of a given note one half step*. A **flat** (♭) is *a symbol that lowers the pitch of a given note one half step*. A **natural** (♮) is *a symbol that cancels a previous sharp or flat, or a sharp or flat in a key signature*. An **accidental** (another name for an altered pitch) is *any sharp, flat or natural that is not included in the key signature of a piece of music*.

◆ The Natural Minor Scale

The **natural minor scale** is *a minor scale that uses no altered pitches or accidentals*. Play the A natural minor scale on the piano, and sing the scale using solfège syllables.

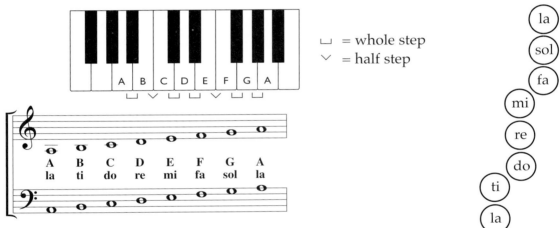

◆ The Harmonic Minor Scale

The **harmonic minor scale** is *a minor scale that uses a raised seventh note*, si *(raised from* sol*)*. The seventh note is also known as the leading tone, since it creates a strong feeling of motion toward the tonic, or *la*. Play the A harmonic minor scale on the piano, and sing the scale using solfège syllables.

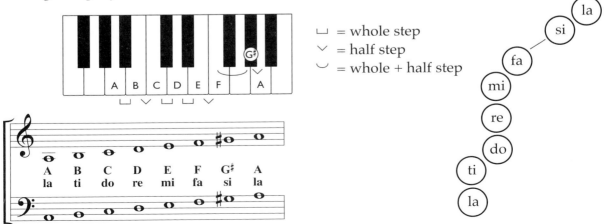

◆ The Melodic Minor Scale

The **melodic minor scale** is *a minor scale that uses raised sixth and seventh notes*, fi *(raised from* fa*) and* si *(raised from* sol*)*. Often, these notes are raised in ascending patterns, but not in descending patterns. Play the A melodic minor scale on the piano, and sing the scale using solfège syllables.

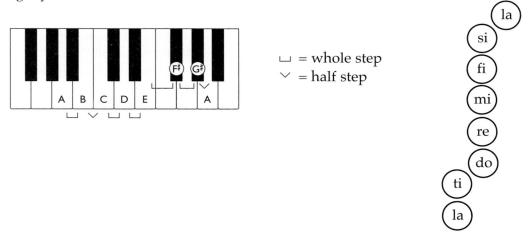

⊔ = whole step
∨ = half step

A   B   C   D   E   F♯   G♯   A   G♮   F♮   E   D   C   B   A
la ti do re mi fi   si   la sol fa mi re do ti la

◆ Practice

Sight-sing the following exercises that use altered pitches or accidentals.

1 Harmonic Minor

la   si

2 Melodic Minor

mi   fi si

Practice

◆ Pitch and Rhythm • A Minor Tonic and Dominant Chords

Using the A minor patterns below as a guide, sight-sing the following exercises separately or in any combination.

Come And Be Merry

Words and Music by
AUDREY SNYDER

Rhythm

◆ Tied Notes

A **tie** is *a curved line used to connect two or more notes of the same pitch in order to make one longer note.*

◆ Practice

Sight-sing the following exercises that use tied notes.

Evaluation

Demonstrate what you have learned in Chapter Three by completing the following:

◆ **Major Tonic**
1. In major keys, tonic chords consist of which three solfège syllables?
2. What are the letter names of the notes of the C major tonic chord?

◆ **Minor Tonic**
1. In minor keys, tonic chords consist of which three solfège syllables?
2. What are the letter names of the notes of the A minor tonic chord?

◆ Name these kinds of notes and rests.

◆ **Musical Math**
When the quarter note receives the beat, are each of these equations true or false?

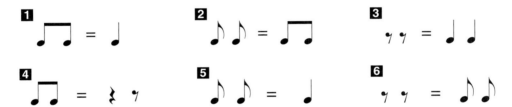

◆ Sight-sing the following exercises.

Evaluation

◆ ## The Three Minor Scales

1. Name the notes in the A natural minor scale. What are the solfège syllables?
2. To alter the natural minor scale to make it an ascending melodic minor scale, the sixth and the seventh notes of the scale must be raised one half step. *Fa* becomes what syllable? *Sol* becomes what syllable?
3. The harmonic minor scale has a raised seventh tone (*si* from *sol*). In the A harmonic minor scale, what is the note name of *si*?

◆ ## True or False?

1. In both major and minor keys, dominant chords are built on the third note of the scale.
2. In the key of C major, the dominant chord is built on G.

◆ Answer the following questions:

1. In major keys, dominant chords consist of which three solfège syllables?
2. What are the letter names of the notes of the C major dominant chord?
3. In natural minor keys, dominant chords consist of which three solfège syllables?
4. In harmonic minor keys, dominant chords consist of which three solfège syllables?

◆ Sight-sing the following exercises.

Pitch

◆ The F Major Scale

A **flat** (♭) is *a symbol that lowers the pitch of a given note one half step.* The note to the right, B♭ (B flat), is written with the flat sign to the left of the notehead.

The major scale is a specific arrangement of whole steps and half steps:

W + W + H + W + W + W + H

The F major scale is a major scale that starts and ends on F. To build this scale, begin on F and use the pattern of whole steps and half steps shown above. Notice the need for a B♭. Play the F major scale on the piano.

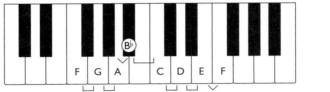

⌐ = whole step
∨ = half step

Sing the F major scale using solfège syllables. Where do the whole steps occur? Where do the half steps occur?

◆ Key Signature

The **key signature** is *a symbol or set of symbols that determines the key of a piece of music.* In the key of F major, there will always be a B♭. Rather than write a flat sign on every B in a piece of music, a flat is placed on the B line of the staff at the beginning of the piece, to the right of the clef sign.

The key signature for F major looks like this:

◆ Practice

Read and echo the following examples to practice singing notes from the F major scale.

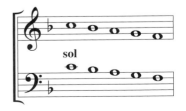

Pitch

◆ The F Major Tonic and Dominant Chords

The **tonic chord** is *a chord built on the home tone, or keynote, of a scale.* In a major scale, this chord uses the notes *do, mi* and *sol* and is sometimes called the **I** ("one") chord, since it is based on the first note of the scale, or *do.* The **dominant chord** is *a chord built on the fifth note of a scale.* In a major scale, this chord uses the notes *sol, ti* and *re* and is sometimes called the **V** ("five") chord, since it is based on the fifth note of the scale, or *sol.*

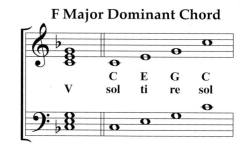

◆ Practice

Using the F major patterns above as a guide, sight-sing the following exercises separately or in any combination.

Green Grows The Willow

Words and Music by
EMILY CROCKER

dar - ling, will you be mine? Green grows the wil-low tree.

dar - ling, will you be mine? Green grows the wil-low tree.

dar - ling, will you be mine? Green grows the wil-low tree.

dar - ling, will you be mine? Green grows the wil-low tree.

Soft is the grass. Sweet is the day for a lad-die and a lass.

Soft is the grass. Sweet is the day for a lad-die and a lass.

Soft is the grass. Sweet is the day for a lad-die and a lass.

Soft is the grass. Sweet is the day for a lad-die and a lass.

*Second time observe fermatas

Rhythm

◆ Reviewing Tied Notes

A **tie** is *a curved line used to connect two or more notes of the same pitch in order to make one longer note.* For example, two quarter notes tied together equal one half note.

◆ Practice

Clap, tap, or chant while conducting the following exercises that use tied notes.

1
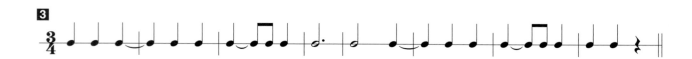

2

3

4

Sight-sing the following exercises that use tied notes.

5

do

6

sol

Rhythm

◆ Dotted Half and Dotted Quarter Notes

A **dot** is *a symbol that increases the length of a given note by half its value.* It is placed to the right of the note.

When the quarter note receives the beat:

A dotted half note receives three beats (the same as a half note tied to a quarter note).

A dotted quarter note receives one and a half beats (the same as a quarter note tied to an eighth note).

Dotted rhythms are often combinations of unequal note values. For example, a longer dotted note is sometimes followed by a shorter note.

◆ Practice

Clap, tap or chant while conducting the following exercises that use dotted half and dotted quarter notes.

1

2

Sight-sing the following exercises that use dotted half and dotted quarter notes.

3

4

Terms and Symbols

◆ Dynamics

Sight-sing and practice this two-part speech chorus. Make your performance more interesting by using **dynamics**, or *symbols in music used to indicate how loud or soft to sing.* See the box on the right for a quick guide to dynamics.

p	= piano (soft)
mp	= mezzo piano (medium soft)
mf	= mezzo forte (medium loud)
f	= forte (loud)
ff	= fortissimo (very loud)
<	= crescendo (get louder)
>	= decrescendo (get softer)

SIGHT-SING

Match Cats Road Trip

Words and Music by
EMILY CROCKER

Practice

◆ Pitch and Rhythm • Dotted Notes in F Major

Using the F major patterns below as a guide, sight-sing the following sets of exercises separately or in any combination.

F Major Scale

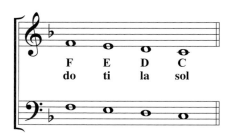

Exercises in 3/4 Meter

Exercises in 4/4 Meter

Proverb

Anonymous

Music by EMILY CROCKER

Pitch

◆ The D Minor Scale

The minor scale is a specific arrangement of whole steps and half steps:

$$W \; + \; H \; + \; W \; + \; W \; + \; H \; + \; W \; + \; W$$

The D minor scale is a minor scale that starts and ends on D. To build this scale, begin on D and use the pattern of whole steps and half steps shown above. Notice the need for a B♭. Play the D minor scale on the piano.

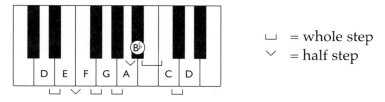

⌐⌐ = whole step
⌄ = half step

Sing the D minor scale using solfège syllables. Where do the whole steps occur? Where do the half steps occur?

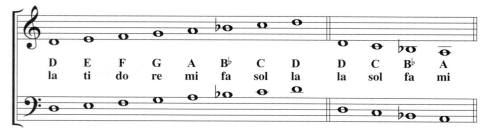

D	E	F	G	A	B♭	C	D	D	C	B♭	A
la	ti	do	re	mi	fa	sol	la	la	sol	fa	mi

The D minor scale is called the relative minor of the F major scale, since both scales have the same half steps (E and F, *ti* and *do;* A and B♭, *mi* and *fa*).

◆ Key Signature

In the key of D minor, there will always be a B♭. The key signature for D minor looks like this:

◆ Practice

Sight-sing the following exercise in D minor.

la

Pitch

◆ The D Minor Tonic and Dominant Chords

The **tonic chord** is *a chord built on the home tone, or keynote, of a scale.* In a minor scale, this chord uses the notes *la, do* and *mi* and is sometimes called the **i** ("one") chord, since it is based on the first note of the scale, or *la.*

The **dominant chord** is *a chord built on the fifth note of a scale.* In a minor scale, this chord uses the notes *mi, sol* and *ti* (or *mi, si* and *ti*) and is sometimes called the **v** or **V** ("five") chord, since it is based on the fifth note of the scale, or *mi.*

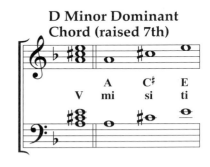

◆ Practice

Using the D minor patterns above as a guide, sight-sing the following exercises separately or in any combination.

My Peace

Words and Music by
EMILY CROCKER

Evaluation

Demonstrate what you have learned in Chapter Four by completing the following:

◆ Musical Math

When the quarter note receives the beat:

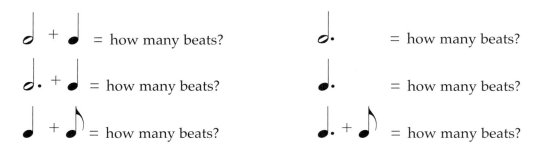

♩ + ♩ = how many beats?   ♩. = how many beats?

♩. + ♩ = how many beats?   ♩. = how many beats?

♩ + ♪ = how many beats?   ♩. + ♪ = how many beats?

◆ Clap, tap or chant the following exercises.

1

2

◆ Sight-sing the following melody.

German Melody

la

CHAPTER 5

Rhythm

◆ Sixteenth Notes

The **beat** is *the steady pulse of all music.* **Rhythm** is *the combination of long and short notes and rests.*

A **sixteenth note** is *a note that represents one quarter beat of sound when the quarter note receives the beat.* Four sixteenth notes equal one beat of sound when the quarter note receives the beat.

Sixteenth Notes

◆ Practice

Clap, tap or chant the following exercises to practice reading sixteenth notes.

Rhythm

◆ Sixteenth and Eighth Note Combinations

A **sixteenth note** is *a note that represents one quarter beat of sound when the quarter note receives the beat.* Four sixteenth notes equal one beat of sound when the quarter note receives the beat. Sixteenth notes can be combined with a variety of notes. Often, sixteenth notes are combined with eighth notes and eighth rests.

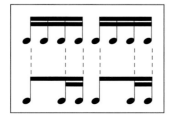

Note Combinations

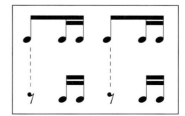

Note and Rest Combinations

◆ Practice

Clap, tap or chant while conducting the following exercises to practice reading sixteenth and eighth note combinations. Keep the beat steady.

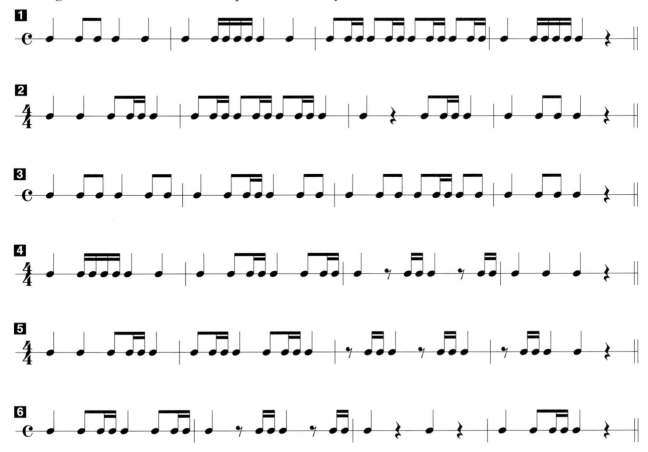

Rhythm

◆ More Sixteenth and Eighth Note Combinations

Sixteenth notes can be combined with a variety of notes. Often, sixteenth notes are combined with eighth notes and eighth rests.

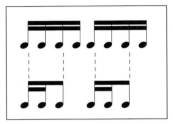

Note Combinations

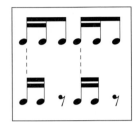

Note and Rest Combinations

◆ Practice

Clap, tap or chant while conducting the following exercises to practice reading sixteenth and eighth note combinations.

Restaurante Mexicano

Words and Music by
AUDREY SNYDER

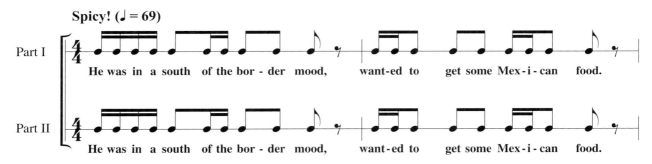

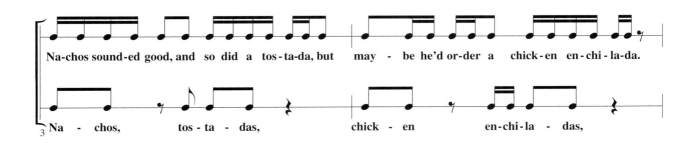

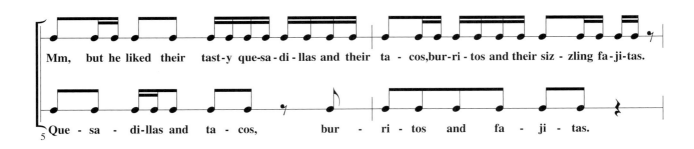

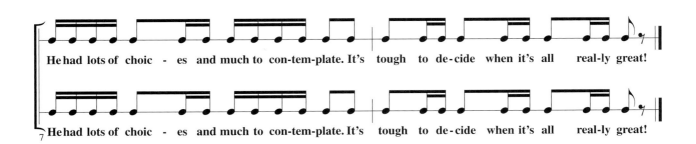

Rhythm

◆ Time Signature • $\frac{2}{4}$ Meter

$\frac{2}{4}$ **meter** is *a time signature in which there are two beats per measure and the quarter note receives the beat.* A whole rest ▬ in $\frac{2}{4}$ meter represents one measure of silence.

2 = two beats per measure
4 = the quarter note receives the beat

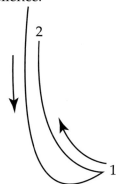

Study and practice the conducting pattern to the right.

◆ Practice

Chant the rhythms in the following exercises as you conduct.

Practice

◆ Pitch and Rhythm • D Minor in $\frac{2}{4}$ Meter

Using the D minor patterns below as a guide, sight-sing the following exercises separately or in any combination.

Jubilate
Sing Joyfully

Words and Music by
AUDREY SNYDER

* Sopranos and Tenors sing notes with the stems up. Altos and Basses sing notes with the stems down.

*All parts sing the same notes in unison, regardless of stem direction.

Pitch

The G Major Scale

A **sharp** is *a symbol that raises the pitch of a given note one half step.* The note to the right, F♯ (F sharp), is written with the sharp sign to the left of the notehead.

The major scale is a specific arrangement of whole steps and half steps: W + W + H + W + W + W + H.

The G major scale is a major scale that starts and ends on G. To build this scale, begin on G and use the pattern of whole steps and half steps shown above. Notice the need for an F♯. Play the G major scale on the piano.

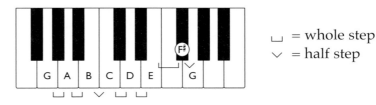

⊔ = whole step
⌄ = half step

Sing the G major scale using solfège syllables. Where do the whole steps occur? Where do the half steps occur?

Key Signature

In the key of G major, there will always be an F♯. The key signature for G major looks like this:

Practice

Read and echo the following exercises to practice singing notes from the G major scale.

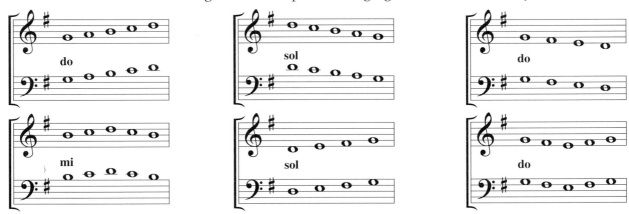

Pitch

◆ The G Major Tonic, Dominant and Subdominant Chords

The **tonic chord** is *a chord built on the home tone, or keynote, of a scale.* The **dominant chord** is *a chord built on the fifth note of a scale.* The **subdominant chord** is *a chord built on the fourth note of a scale.* In a major scale, this chord uses the notes *fa, la* and *do* and is sometimes called the **IV** ("four") chord, since it is based on the fourth note of the scale, or *fa*.

**G Major
Tonic Chord**

**G Major
Dominant Chord**

**G Major
Subdominant Chord**

◆ Practice

Read and echo the following examples to practice intervals found in the G major tonic and dominant chords.

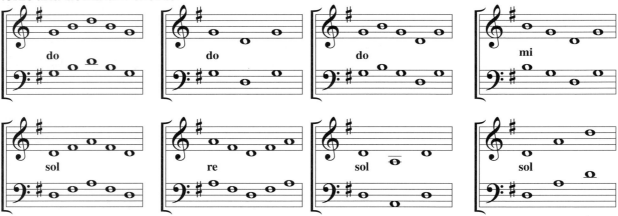

Read and echo the following examples to practice intervals found in the G major subdominant chord.

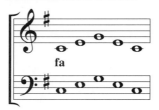

Practice

◆ Pitch and Rhythm • G Major Tonic, Dominant and Subdominant Chords

Using the G major patterns below as a guide, sight-sing the following sets of exercises separately or in any combination.

Morning

Pawnee Prayer, adapted

Music by
AUDREY SNYDER

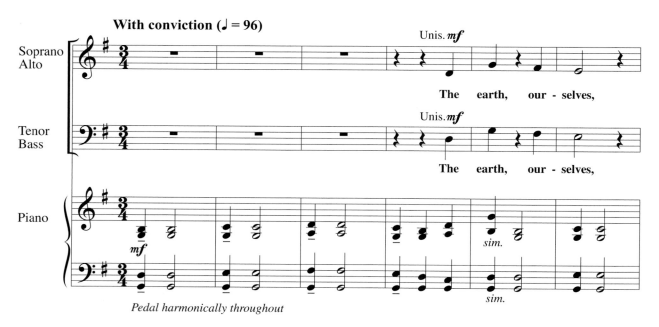

*Sopranos and Tenors sing the top notes; Altos and Basses sing the bottom notes, regardless of stem direction.

Rhythm

◆ Dotted Eighth and Sixteenth Note Combinations

Dotted rhythms are often combinations of unequal note values. For example, a longer dotted note is sometimes followed by a shorter note.

The rhythm pattern to the right uses dotted eighth notes followed by sixteenth notes. This rhythm is a "long-short" pattern.

Sometimes a shorter note is followed by a longer dotted note.

The rhythmic pattern to the right uses sixteenth notes followed by dotted eighth notes. This is a "short-long" pattern.

◆ Practice

Clap, tap or chant while conducting the following exercises that use dotted eighth and sixteenth note combinations.

Practice

◆ Pitch and Rhythm • Dotted Eighth and Sixteenth Notes in G Major

Using the G major patterns below as a guide, sight-sing the following exercises separately or in any combination.

Pitch

◆ The E Minor Scale

The minor scale is a specific arrangement of whole steps and half steps:

$$W + H + W + W + H + W + W$$

The E minor scale is a minor scale that starts and ends on E. To build this scale, begin on E and use the pattern of whole steps and half steps shown above. Notice the need for an F♯. Play the E minor scale on the piano.

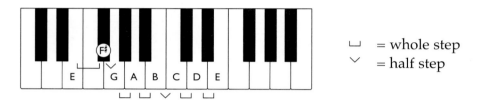

= whole step
= half step

Sing the E minor scale using solfège syllables. Where do the whole steps occur? Where do the half steps occur?

The E minor scale is called the relative minor of the G major scale, since both scales have the same half steps (F♯ and G, *ti* and *do*; B and C, *mi* and *fa*).

◆ Key Signature

In the key of E minor, there will always be an F♯. The key signature for E minor looks like this:

◆ Practice

Read and echo the following exercises to practice singing notes from the E minor scale.

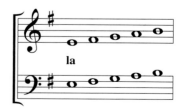

Pitch

◆ The E Minor Tonic, Dominant and Subdominant Chords

The **tonic chord** is *a chord built on the home tone, or keynote, of a scale.* The **dominant chord** is *a chord built on the fifth note of a scale.* The **subdominant chord** is *a chord built on the fourth note of a scale.* In a minor scale, this chord uses the notes *re, fa* and *la,* and is sometimes called the **iv** ("four") chord, since it is based on the fourth note of the scale, or *re.*

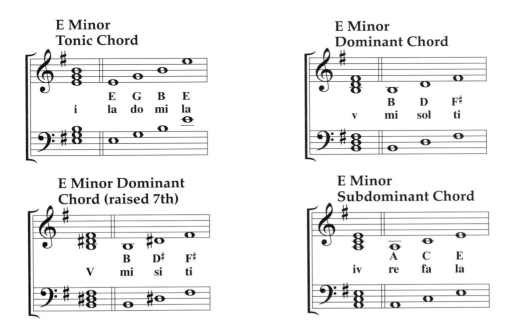

◆ Practice

Read and echo the following exercises to practice singing intervals found in the E minor tonic, dominant and subdominant chords.

Practice

◆ Pitch and Rhythm • E Minor Tonic, Dominant and Subdominant Chords

Using the E minor patterns below as a guide, sight-sing the following exercises separately or in any combination.

Sail On, Clipper Ship

Noted for their speed, clipper ships were slender,
many-sailed vessels that were used to
transport passengers and cargo in the mid-1800s.

Words and Music by
AUDREY SNYDER

Evaluation

Demonstrate what you have learned in Chapter Five by completing the following:

◆ **Musical Math**

When the quarter note receives the beat, do these rhythm patterns each equal the same amount of time?

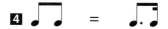

◆ In $\frac{2}{4}$ meter, how many beats are there per measure? Which kind of note receives the beat?

◆ Clap, tap or chant while conducting.

◆ Answer the following questions:
1. In a major scale, the dominant chord is built on which note of the scale? Which solfège syllable?
2. In a major scale, the subdominant chord is built on which note of the scale? Which solfège syllable?
3. In a natural, melodic or harmonic minor scale, the dominant chord is built on which note of the scale? Which solfège syllable?
4. In a natural, melodic or harmonic minor scale, the subdominant chord is built on which note of the scale? Which solfège syllable?

◆ Sight-sing the following exercises. Which one is in G major? Which one is in E minor?

CHAPTER 6

Terms and Symbols

◆ Accent >

An **accent** is *a symbol placed above or below a given note that indicates the note should receive extra emphasis or stress.*

Accented Notes

In order to establish the feel of the meter, it is important to stress the first beat of the measure. Sight-sing the following exercise, placing stress on the accented notes.

1

◆ Syncopation

Syncopation *occurs when the accent is placed on notes that normally do not receive extra emphasis.* Syncopation can be found in all types of music.

◆ Practice

Read and echo the following examples to practice rhythms with syncopation.

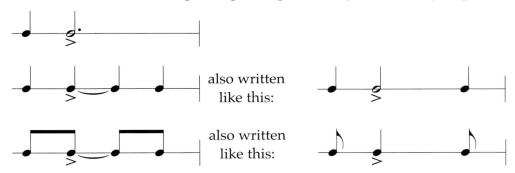

also written like this:

also written like this:

Clap, tap or chant while conducting the following exercises to practice reading rhythms with syncopation.

2

3

Practice

◆ Pitch and Rhythm • Syncopation in E Minor
Clap, tap or chant while conducting the syncopated rhythm pattern below.

Using the E minor patterns below as a guide, sight-sing the following exercises separately or in any combination.

Blessed Song Of Peace

Words and Music by
EMILY CROCKER

Pitch

◆ The Key of B♭ Major

The B♭ major scale is a major scale that starts and ends on B♭. To play a B♭ major scale on the piano, begin on B♭ and use the pattern of whole steps and half steps for a major scale. The B♭ major scale has two flats in its key signature: B♭ and E♭.

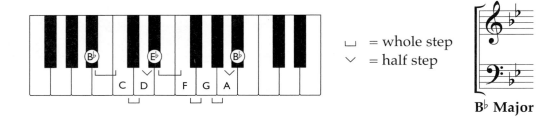

⌐ = whole step
∨ = half step

B♭ Major

◆ Practice

Sing the B♭ major scale and chord patterns.

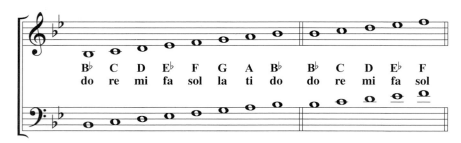

| B♭ | C | D | E♭ | F | G | A | B♭ | B♭ | C | D | E♭ | F |
| do | re | mi | fa | sol | la | ti | do | do | re | mi | fa | sol |

B♭ Major Tonic Chord Pattern

B♭ D F B♭ F D B♭
do mi sol do sol mi do

B♭ Major Dominant Chord Pattern

F A C A F C F
sol ti re ti sol re sol

B♭ Major Subdominant Chord Pattern

E♭ G B♭ G E♭ B♭ E♭
fa la do la fa do fa

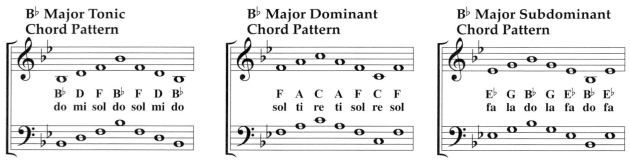

Sight-sing the following exercise in B♭ major.

do

Pitch

◆ The B♭ Major Tonic, Dominant and Subdominant Chords

In tonal music, a **triad** is *a chord built in thirds over a root tone or note.* The **tonic chord (I)** is *a chord built on the home tone, or keynote, of a scale.* The **dominant chord (V)** is *a chord built on the fifth note of a scale.* The **subdominant chord (IV)** is *a chord built on the fourth note of a scale.*

B♭ Major Tonic Chord

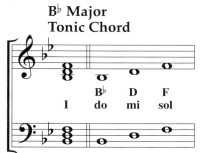

I	B♭	D	F
	do	mi	sol

B♭ Major Dominant Chord

V	F	A	C	F
	sol	ti	re	sol

B♭ Major Subdominant Chord

IV	E♭	G	B♭	E♭
	fa	la	do	fa

◆ Primary Chords

The tonic, dominant and subdominant chords are called primary chords and are related in the way that they interact with each other. Some descriptions of these primary chords include:

- **Tonic (I)** - home, at ease, rest
- **Subdominant (IV)** - digression, movement away from the tonic
- **Dominant (V)** - energy, momentum toward the tonic

Identify each chord below as I, IV or V. Then, sing each chord drill and listen to the relationships between each chord.

1

2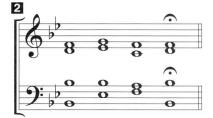

3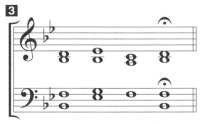

◆ Practice

Sight-sing the following melody that uses pitches found in the B♭ major tonic, dominant and subdominant chords.

Practice

◆ Pitch and Rhythm • B♭ Major Tonic, Dominant and Subdominant Chords

Using the B♭ major patterns below as a guide, sing the following chord drills. Then sight-sing the exercises separately or in any combination.

Pitch

◆ The B♭ Major Diatonic Chords

The primary chords in tonal music are the tonic, subdominant and dominant chords. In the major scale, these chords are major chords.

Chords can be built on the four remaining notes of the major scale. These four chords, plus the primary chords, are called diatonic chords, because no accidentals are used.

B♭ Major Diatonic Chords

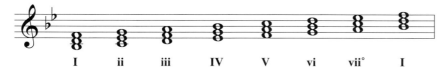

I   ii   iii   IV   V   vi   vii°   I

Play the above chords on the piano and listen to the harmony of each chord.
- **Major chord:** I, IV, V
- **Minor chord:** ii, iii, vi
- **Diminished chord:** vii°

◆ B♭ Major Chord Patterns and Substitutions

The remaining diatonic chords also have names:

ii = **supertonic chord** *(the chord immediately above the tonic)*

iii = **mediant chord** *(the chord midway between the tonic and the dominant)*

vi = **submediant chord** *(the chord below the tonic, midway between it and the dominant)*

vii° = **leading tone** *(the tone and chord in the scale that has the strongest progression toward the tonic)*

◆ Practice

The boxed chords can be substituted for the tonic, subdominant and dominant chords. Identify each chord below. Then sing each chord drill.

1

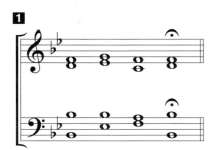

2

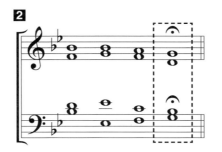

3

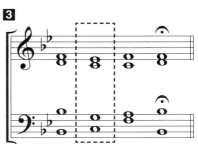

Deo Gratias

Words and Music by
EMILY CROCKER

Pitch

◆ The Key of G Minor

The G minor scale is a minor scale that starts and ends on G. To play a G minor scale on the piano, begin on G and use the pattern of whole steps and half steps for a minor scale. The G minor scale has two flats in its key signature: B♭ and E♭, and is the relative minor of B♭ major.

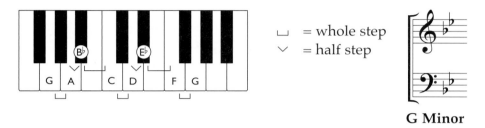

◆ Practice

Sing the G minor scales and chord patterns.

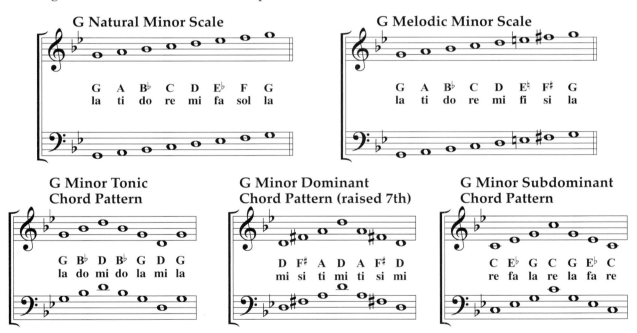

Sight-sing the following exercise in G minor.

Pitch

◆ The G Minor Tonic, Dominant and Subdominant Chords

In tonal music, a triad is a chord built in thirds over a root tone or note. The **tonic chord** is *a chord built on the home tone, or keynote, of a scale.* The **dominant chord** is *a chord built on the fifth note of a scale.* The **subdominant chord** is *a chord built on the fourth note of a scale.*

G Minor
Tonic Chord

G Minor Dominant
Chord (raised 7th)

G Minor
Subdominant Chord

◆ Practice

Identify each chord below as I, IV or V. Then sing each chord drill and listen to the relationship between each chord.

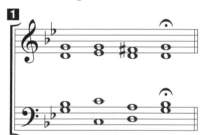

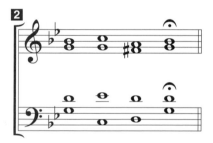

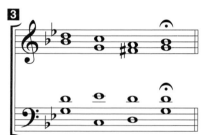

Sight-sing the following exercises separately or in any combination.

Practice

◆ Pitch and Rhythm • G Minor Tonic, Dominant and Subdominant Chords

Using the G minor patterns below as a guide, sight-sing the following exercises separately or in any combination.

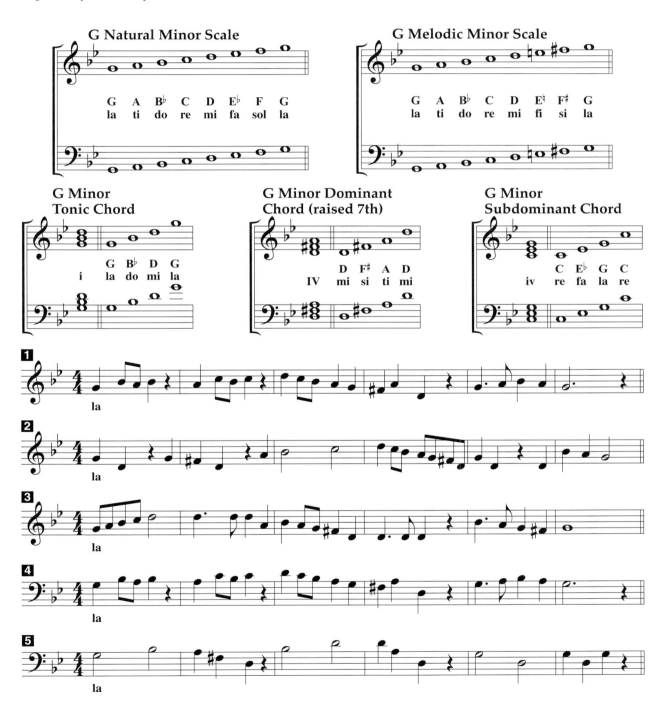

Let The Bullgine Run

Sea Chantey

Music by
EMILY CROCKER

Pitch

◆ The Key of D Major

The D major scale is a major scale that starts and ends on D. To play a D major scale on the piano, begin on D and use the pattern of whole steps and half steps for a major scale. The D major scale has two sharps in its key signature: F♯ and C♯.

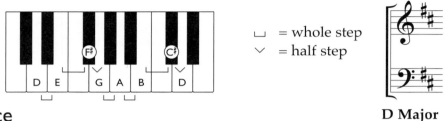

= whole step
= half step

D Major

◆ Practice

Sing the D major scale and chord patterns.

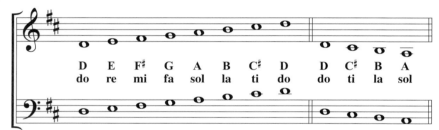

| D | E | F♯ | G | A | B | C♯ | D | D | C♯ | B | A |
| do | re | mi | fa | sol | la | ti | do | do | ti | la | sol |

D Major Tonic Chord Pattern

D Major Dominant Chord Pattern

D Major Subdominant Chord Pattern

D F♯ A D A F♯ D
do mi sol do sol mi do

A C♯ E C♯ A E A
sol ti re ti sol re sol

G B D B G D G
fa la do la fa do fa

Sight-sing the following exercise in D major.

do

Pitch

◆ The D Major Diatonic Chords

Play the following diatonic chords on the piano. Which chords are major? Which are minor? Which are diminished?

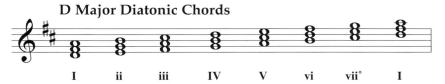

D Major Diatonic Chords

I   ii   iii   IV   V   vi   vii°   I

Diatonic chords can be substituted for each other in order to create harmonic interest. See the categories of harmony described in the chart below.

TONIC	SUBDOMINANT	DOMINANT
home, at ease, rest	digression, movement away from the tonic	momentum, motion toward the tonic
I (vi, iii)	IV (ii)	V (vii°, iii)

◆ Practice

Identify each chord below. Then, sing each chord drill.

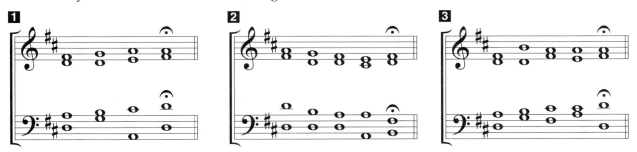

Sight-sing the following melody in D major.

Practice

◆ Pitch and Rhythm • D Major Diatonic Chords

Using the D major patterns below as a guide, sight-sing the following exercises separately or in any combination.

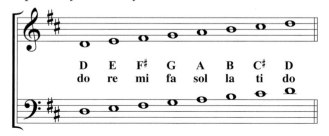 

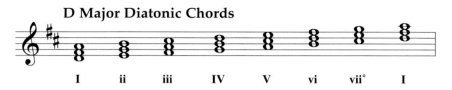

Rhythm

◆ Mixed Meter

Mixed meter is *a technique in which the time signature or meter changes frequently within a piece of music.*

In $\frac{2}{4}$, $\frac{3}{4}$ and $\frac{4}{4}$ meters, the quarter note beat remains the same, but the number of beats per measure changes.

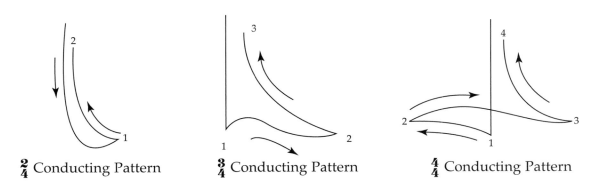

$\frac{2}{4}$ Conducting Pattern $\frac{3}{4}$ Conducting Pattern $\frac{4}{4}$ Conducting Pattern

◆ Practice

Using the conducting patterns above as a guide, chant the rhythms in the following exercise. Keep the beat steady.

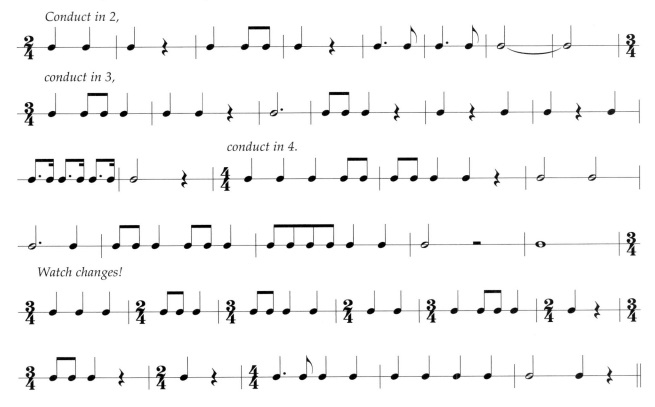

Match Cats Bebop

Words and Music by
EMILY CROCKER

Brothers and Sisters

Words and Music by
EMILY CROCKER

Last time to Coda ⊕ (m. 23)

out the land, al - le - lu - ia. al - le - lu - ia.

night and day, al - le - lu - ia. al - le - lu - ia.

le - lu - ia. lu - ia.

le - lu - ia. lu - ia.

Last time to Coda ⊕ (m. 23)

Al - le - lu - ia.

Al - le - lu - ia, sing with praise, sing with praise.

Al - le - lu - ia.

Al - le - lu - ia, sing with praise, sing with praise.

Evaluation

Demonstrate what you have learned in Chapter Six by completing the following:

◆ Be A Composer

Create a rhythm composition that uses syncopated patterns. Each of the following patterns equals two beats in $\frac{2}{4}$ meter. Copy the staff below onto a sheet of paper. Arrange the rhythm patterns below in any order you wish in the six measures.

Clap or play your rhythm composition on a percussion instrument, or add pitches and sing or play on a melody instrument.

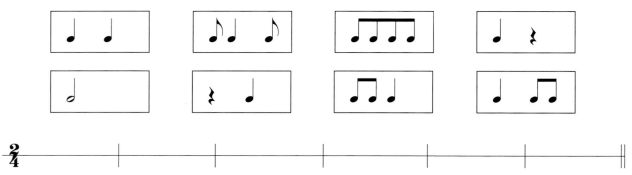

◆ Primary and Diatonic Chords

Identify the chords below using both the chord number and name.

Primary Chords
- Tonic (I)
- Subdominant (IV)
- Dominant (V)

Diatonic Chords
- Tonic (I)
- Supertonic (ii)
- Mediant (iii)
- Subdominant (IV)
- Dominant (V)
- Submediant (vi)
- Leading tone (vii°)

Key of B♭ Major

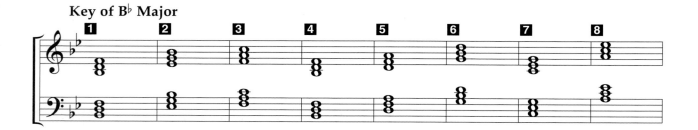

Rhythm

◆ Simple Meter and Compound Meter

The **beat** is *the steady pulse of all music.* **Simple meter** is *any meter in which the quarter note receives the beat, and the division of the beat is based on two eighth notes.* $\frac{2}{4}$, $\frac{3}{4}$ and $\frac{4}{4}$ meters are examples of simple meter.

2 = two beats per measure
4 = the quarter note receives the beat

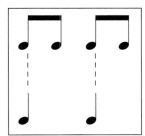

Compound meter is *any meter in which the dotted quarter note receives the beat, and the division of the beat is based on three eighth notes.* $\frac{6}{8}$ meter is an example of compound meter.

6 = two groups of three eighth notes per measure
8 = the dotted quarter note receives the beat

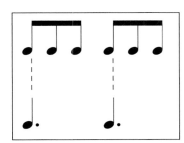

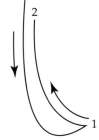

Like $\frac{2}{4}$, $\frac{6}{8}$ meter is usually conducted in two (except when the tempo is very slow).

◆ Practice

Chant the rhythms of the following exercises as you conduct.

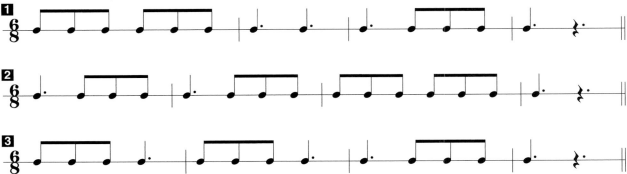

Rhythm

◆ Time Signature • $\frac{6}{8}$ Meter

Compound meter is *any meter in which the dotted quarter note receives the beat, and the division of the beat is based on three eighth notes.* $\frac{6}{8}$ meter is an example of compound meter. The following rhythms are all common in $\frac{6}{8}$ meter.

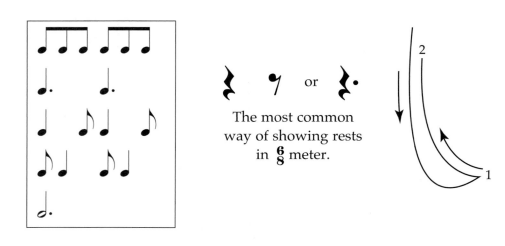

The most common way of showing rests in $\frac{6}{8}$ meter.

◆ Practice

$\frac{6}{8}$ meter is usually conducted in two, unless the tempo is very slow. Clap, tap or chant while conducting the following exercises to practice reading rhythms in $\frac{6}{8}$ meter.

Pitch

◆ The Key of E♭ Major

The E♭ major scale is a major scale that starts and ends on E♭. To play an E♭ major scale on the piano, begin on E♭ and use the pattern of whole steps and half steps for a major scale. The E♭ major scale has three flats in its key signature: B♭, E♭ and A♭.

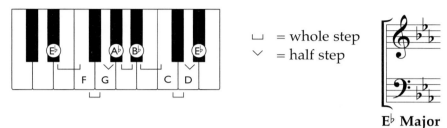

◆ Practice

Sing the E♭ major scale and chord patterns.

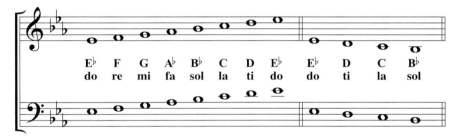

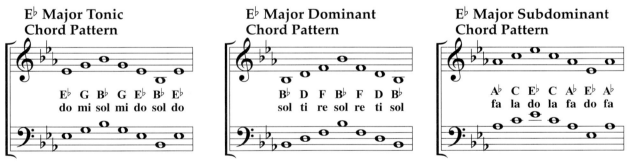

Sight-sing the following exercises in E♭ major.

Practice

◆ Pitch and Rhythm • E♭ Major Tonic, Dominant and Subdominant Chords

E♭ Major
Tonic Chord

I — E♭ G B♭ E♭ — do mi sol do

E♭ Major
Dominant Chord

V — B♭ D F B♭ — sol ti re sol

E♭ Major
Subdominant Chord

IV — A♭ C E♭ A♭ — fa la do fa

Identify each chord below as I, IV or V. Sing each chord drill.

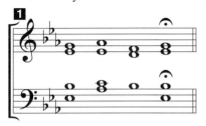

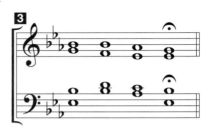

Sight-sing the following exercises separately or in any combination.

Rhythm

◆ Time Signature • $\frac{6}{8}$ and $\frac{9}{8}$ Meter

Simple meter is *any meter in which the quarter note receives the beat and the division of the beat is based on two eighth notes.* **Compound meter** is *any meter in which the dotted quarter note receives the beat and the division of the beat is based on three eighth notes.* $\frac{6}{8}$ and $\frac{9}{8}$ meters are examples of compound meter.

6 = two groups of three eighth notes per measure
8 = the dotted quarter note receives the beat

$\frac{6}{8}$ meter is usually conducted in two, unless the tempo is very slow.

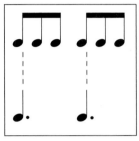 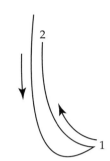

9 = three groups of three eighth notes per measure
8 = the dotted quarter note receives the beat

$\frac{9}{8}$ meter is usually conducted in three.

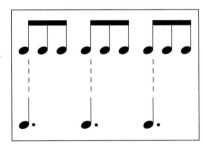 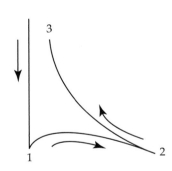

◆ Practice

Chant the rhythms in the following exercises as you conduct.

Rhythm

◆ Time Signature • $\frac{12}{8}$ Meter

$\frac{12}{8}$ meter is another example of compound meter and is usually conducted in four.

12 = four groups of three eighth notes per measure

8 = the dotted quarter note receives the beat

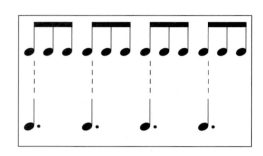

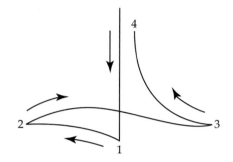

◆ Practice

Chant the rhythms in the following exercises as you conduct.

Crazy Compounds

Challenge! Keep the beat steady.

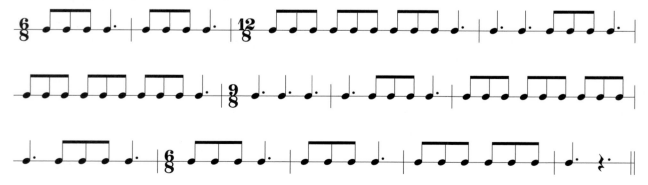

Practice

◆ Pitch and Rhythm • E♭ Major in $\frac{12}{8}$ Meter

Using the E♭ major patterns below as a guide, sight-sing the following exercises separately or in any combination.

E♭ Major
Tonic Chord

I
E♭ G B♭ E♭
do mi sol do

E♭ Major
Dominant Chord

V
B♭ D F B♭
sol ti re sol

E♭ Major
Subdominant Chord

IV
A♭ C E♭ A♭
fa la do fa

◆ Challenge

Conduct in four while you sing.

Summer Day

Words by EMILY BRONTE, adapted

Music by
AUDREY SNYDER

Pitch

◆ The Key of C Minor

The C minor scale is a minor scale that starts and ends on C. To play a C minor scale on the piano, begin on C and use the pattern of whole steps and half steps for a minor scale. The C minor scale has three flats in its key signature: B♭, E♭ and A♭, and is the relative minor of E♭ major.

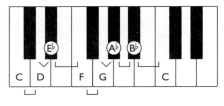

⊔ = whole step
∨ = half step

C Minor

◆ Practice

Sing the C minor scales and chord patterns.

C Natural Minor Scale

C D E♭ F G A♭ B♭ C
la ti do re mi fa sol la

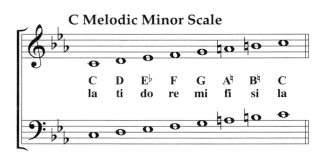

C Melodic Minor Scale

C D E♭ F G A♮ B♮ C
la ti do re mi fi si la

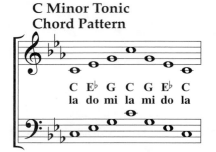

C Minor Tonic
Chord Pattern

C E♭ G C G E♭ C
la do mi la mi do la

C Minor Dominant
Chord Pattern (raised 7th)

G B♮ D B♮ G D G
mi si ti si mi ti mi

C Minor Subdominant
Chord Pattern

F A♭ C A♭ F C F
re fa la fa re la re

Sight-sing the following exercises in C minor.

1

la

2

la

Practice

◆ Pitch and Rhythm • C Minor Tonic, Dominant and Subdominant Chords

Using the C minor patterns below as a guide, sight-sing the following exercises separately or in any combination.

Snowboarders

Words and Music by
AUDREY SNYDER

Down a - cross the moun - tain - side, — deft - ly they cut and turn on a dime.

Snow - board - ers, snow - board - ers, I do not tell a lie; —

Snow - board - ers, snow - board - ers, man, those guys can fly! —

Rhythm

◆ Division of the Beat

Meter is *a way of organizing rhythm.* A meter signature, also called time signature, groups a specific number of beats per measure and assigns a particular note value to receive the beat.

4 = four beats per measure   **3** = three beats per measure
4 = the quarter note receives the beat   **4** = the quarter note receives the beat

2 = two beats per measure   **6** = two groups of three eighth notes per measure
4 = the quarter note receives the beat   **8** = the dotted quarter note receives the beat
                                             (except in a slow tempo)

Music can be grouped according to the beat, or the division of the beat. See the examples below.

Beat

Division of the beat

◆ Practice

With your right hand, conduct the standard four-beat pattern as you chant the exercises below. At the same time, pat the division of the beat (steady eighth notes) on your lap with your left hand.

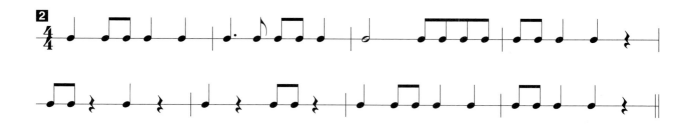

Rhythm

◆ More About Mixed Meter

Sometimes meters will change within a piece of music. When this happens, the number of beats per measure will change based on the top number of the time signature. In $\frac{2}{4}$, $\frac{3}{4}$ and $\frac{4}{4}$ meters, the quarter note beat remains the same, but the number of beats per measure changes.

When $\frac{6}{8}$ meter changes to $\frac{4}{4}$ meter, both the top and bottom numbers are different. Not only does the number of beats per measure change, but so does the kind of note that receives the beat. When this happens, where the meter change occurs, often there will be a tempo equation indicating the relationship between these different note values.

$$(\eighthnote = \eighthnote)$$

◆ Practice

With your left hand, pat a steady eighth note pattern on your lap. At the same time, use your right hand to conduct the beat as indicated as you chant these exercises. Notice that the equation at the meter change indicates that the eighth note value should be kept constant. In other words, the eighth notes should be kept at a steady speed through each meter change.

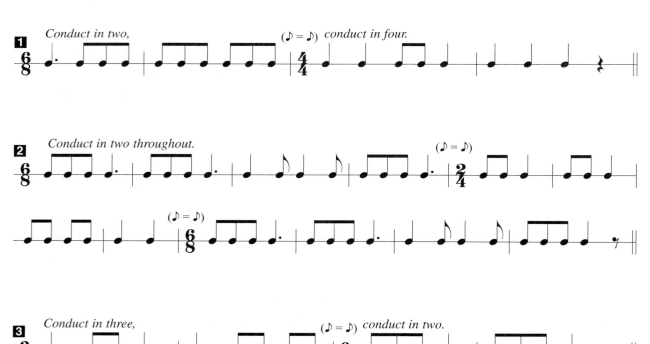

Practice

◆ Rhythm • Mixed Meter Combinations

Clap, tap or chant while conducting the following exercises, keeping the eighth notes at a steady speed throughout each meter change.

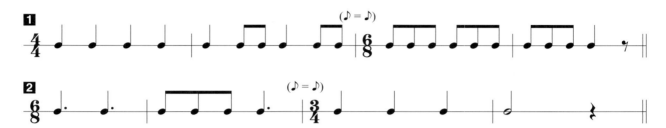

Sometimes the equation will indicate that the beat should be kept constant, rather than the note value. Clap, tap or chant while conducting the following exercises, keeping the beat constant as indicated.

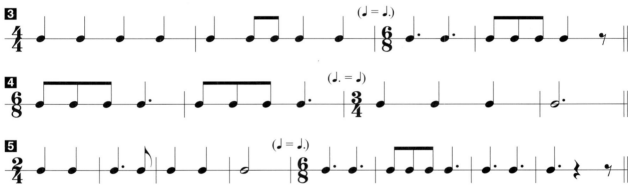

At other times the equation will indicate that neither the beat nor the note values are to remain constant. Clap, tap or chant while conducting the following exercises.

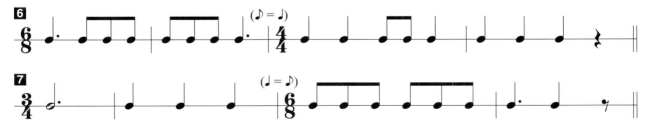

Two English Languages

Words and Music by
AUDREY SNYDER

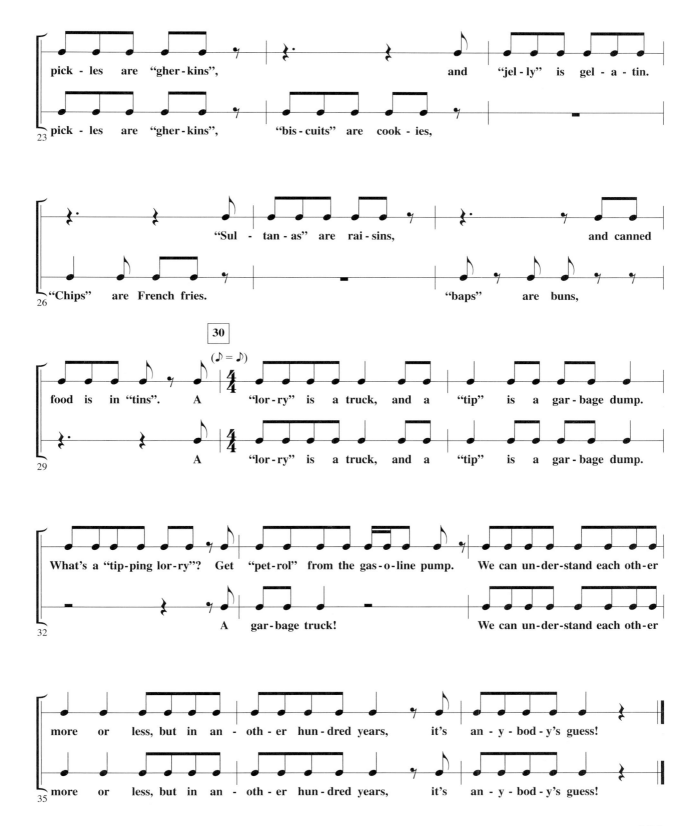

Practice

◆ Mixed Meter in the Time Signature

When specific meter changes occur in a continual pattern throughout a piece of music, these changes are sometimes indicated only in the time signature.

$$\frac{6}{8} + \frac{4}{4} \text{ is sometimes shown simply as } \frac{6}{8}\frac{4}{4}.$$

The above time signature indicates that a measure of $\frac{6}{8}$ meter will be followed by a measure of $\frac{4}{4}$ meter, and these two meters will alternate every measure throughout the piece.

◆ Practice

Clap, tap or chant while conducting the following exercises to practice reading mixed meters.

Practice

◆ Pitch and Rhythm • C Minor in Mixed Meter

Using the C minor patterns below as a guide, sight-sing the following exercises separately or in any combination.

Roll On, River

Words and Music by
AUDREY SNYDER

Evaluation

Demonstrate what you have learned in Chapter Seven by completing the following:

◆ **True or False?**

1. A meter in which the beat is divisible by two is called compound meter.
2. A meter in which the beat is divided into multiples of three is called compound meter.
3. $\frac{2}{4}$, $\frac{3}{4}$ and $\frac{4}{4}$ are simple meters.
4. $\frac{6}{8}$, $\frac{9}{8}$ and $\frac{12}{8}$ are compound meters.

◆ Clap, tap or chant while conducting the following exercises.

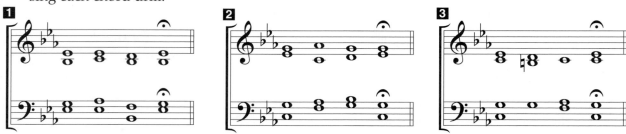

◆ **E♭ Major or C Minor?**

Identify the key of each drill. Then, identify each chord as I, IV, V or i, iv or v. Finally, sing each chord drill.

◆ Conduct as you sight-sing the following exercise, paying special attention to the meter changes.

Identify the key of each exercise below. Sight-sing each exercise.

♦ ## Be a Composer
Compose a complex rhythmic pattern in compound meter. Use the rhythmic patterns learned in this chapter as a guide.

CHAPTER 8

Pitch

◆ The Key of A Major

The A major scale is a major scale that starts and ends on A. To play an A major scale on the piano, begin on A and use the pattern of whole steps and half steps for a major scale. The A major scale has three sharps in its key signature: F♯, C♯ and G♯.

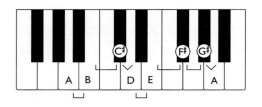
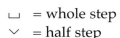

⊔ = whole step
∨ = half step

A Major

◆ Practice

Sing the A major scale and chord patterns.

A	B	C♯	D	E	F♯	G♯	A	A	B	C♯	D	E
do	re	mi	fa	sol	la	ti	do	do	re	mi	fa	sol

A Major Tonic Chord Pattern

A C♯ E A E C♯ A
do mi sol do sol mi do

A Major Dominant Chord Pattern

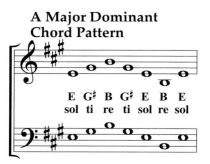

E G♯ B G♯ E B E
sol ti re ti sol re sol

A Major Subdominant Chord Pattern

D F♯ A F♯ D A D
fa la do la fa do fa

Sight-sing the following chord drills.

I IV V I

I IV V vi

I vi ii V I

Practice

◆ Pitch and Rhythm • Key of A Major

Using the A major patterns below as a guide, sight-sing the following exercises separately or in any combination.

Pitch

◆ The Key of F♯ Minor

The F♯ minor scale is a minor scale that starts and ends on F♯. To play an F♯ minor scale on the piano, begin on F♯ and use the pattern of whole steps and half steps for a minor scale. The F♯ minor scale has three sharps in its key signature: F♯, C♯ and G♯, and is the relative minor of A major.

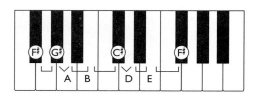

⊔ = whole step
∨ = half step

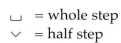

F♯ Minor

◆ Practice

Sing the F♯ minor scales and chord patterns.

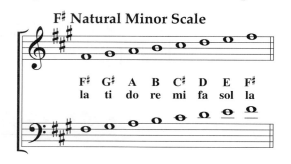

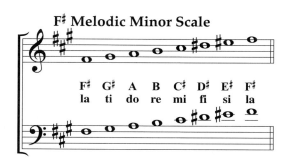

Sight-sing the following chord drills.

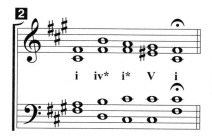

*The keynote (or root of the chord) is not in the bass.

Practice

◆ Pitch and Rhythm • Key of F♯ Minor

Using the F♯ minor patterns on the previous page as a guide, sight-sing the following exercises separately or in any combination.

Irish Blessing

Traditional Irish Text

Music by
EMILY CROCKER

Rhythm

◆ More Simple Meters

Meter is *a way of organizing rhythm.* A meter signature, also called time signature, groups a specific number of beats per measure and assigns a particular note value to receive the beat.

4 = four beats per measure
4 = the quarter note receives the beat

3 = three beats per measure
4 = the quarter note receives the beat

Simple meter is *any meter in which the quarter note receives the beat and the division of the beat is based on two eighth notes.* However, other note values can receive the beat in simple meter, such as the eighth note and half note.

3 = three beats per measure
2 = the half note receives the beat

3 = three beats per measure
8 = the eighth note receives the beat

Music can be grouped according to the beat, or the division or subdivision of the beat. Clap, tap or chant the rhythms in the exercises below. Notice a new rhythmic value in the $\frac{3}{8}$ example. The notes with three beams are called 32nd notes and are created by subdividing the sixteenth notes.

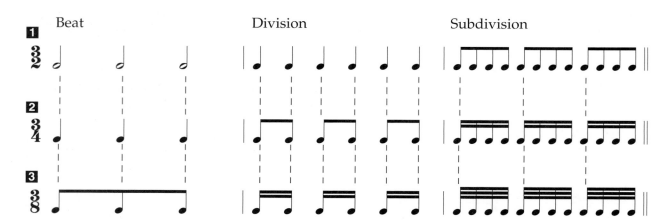

◆ Practice

Clap, tap or chant while conducting the following exercise. Keep the beat constant as indicated between the $\frac{3}{4}$, $\frac{3}{2}$ and $\frac{3}{8}$ meters.

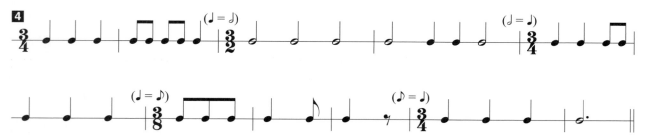

Rhythm

◆ Time Signature • $\frac{2}{2}$ Meter and Cut Time • ₵

Cut time is *another name for* $\frac{2}{2}$ *meter.* In both meters, there are two beats per measure and the half note receives the beat.

◆ Practice

Clap, tap or chant while conducting the following exercise to practice reading rhythms in cut time.

1

Sight-sing the following exercise in cut time.

2

◆ Time Signature • $\frac{3}{2}$ Meter

$\frac{3}{2}$ **meter** is *a time signature in which there are three beats per measure and the half note receives the beat.*

◆ Practice

Clap, tap or chant while conducting the following exercise to practice reading rhythms in $\frac{3}{2}$ meter.

3

Time

Words and Music by
EMILY CROCKER

Time, time, kill-ing time. Time, time, gain-ing time. It's all rel-a-tive.

Unis.

Time, time, wast-ing time. Time, time, kill-ing time, sec-onds, min-utes, hours and days,

Unis.

months, years, de-cades. All — I need is time!

Evaluation

Demonstrate what you have learned in Chapter Eight by completing the following:

◆ **Simple Meters**

Create a rhythm composition that uses different simple meters. Copy the staff below onto a sheet of paper. Arrange the rhythm patterns in any order you wish and repeat as you wish.

Clap your rhythm composition or play it on a percussion instrument. Or, add pitches and sing your composition or play it on a melody instrument.

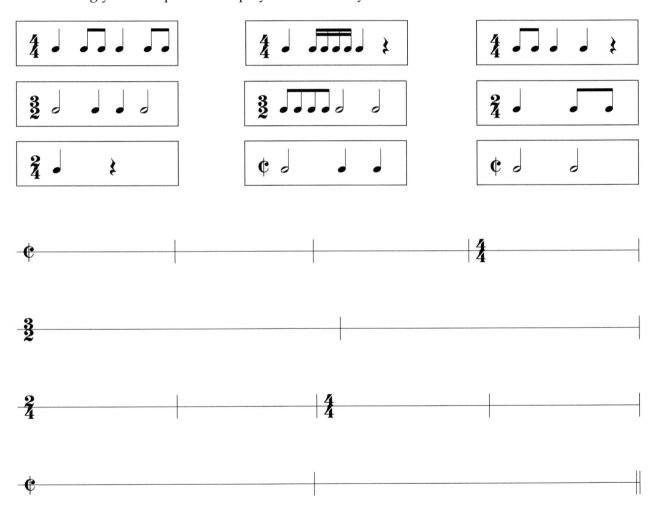

◆ **Challenge**

Create additional rhythm patterns in each meter. Check to see that you have the correct number of beats in each measure.

CHAPTER 9

Pitch

◆ The Circle of Fifths

In music, the relationship between each key is based on a perfect fifth. A **perfect fifth** is *an interval of two pitches that are five notes apart on the staff.* An easy way to visualize this relationship is on the keyboard.

Study the keyboard below. Notice that if you start on C and move to the left by the distance of a fifth, you will find the keys that contain flats. Notice that the number of flats in each key signature increases by one each time you move one perfect fifth to the left.

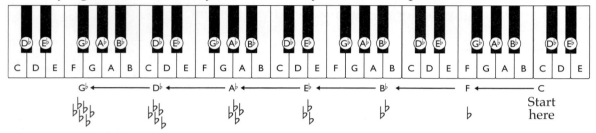

However, if you start on C and move to the right by the distance of a fifth, you will find the keys that contain sharps. Notice that the number of sharps in each key signature increases by one each time you move one perfect fifth to the right.

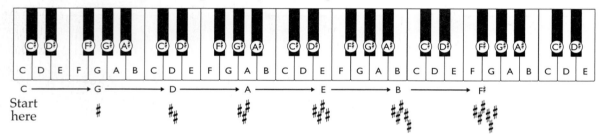

The Circle of Fifths is another easy way to visualize and memorize patterns of sharps, flats and key signatures.

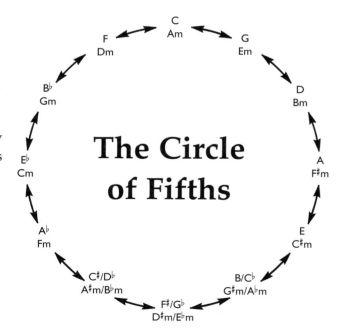

Practice

◆ Pitch and Rhythm • Key of A♭ Major

Using the A♭ major patterns below as a guide, sight-sing the following exercises separately or in any combination.

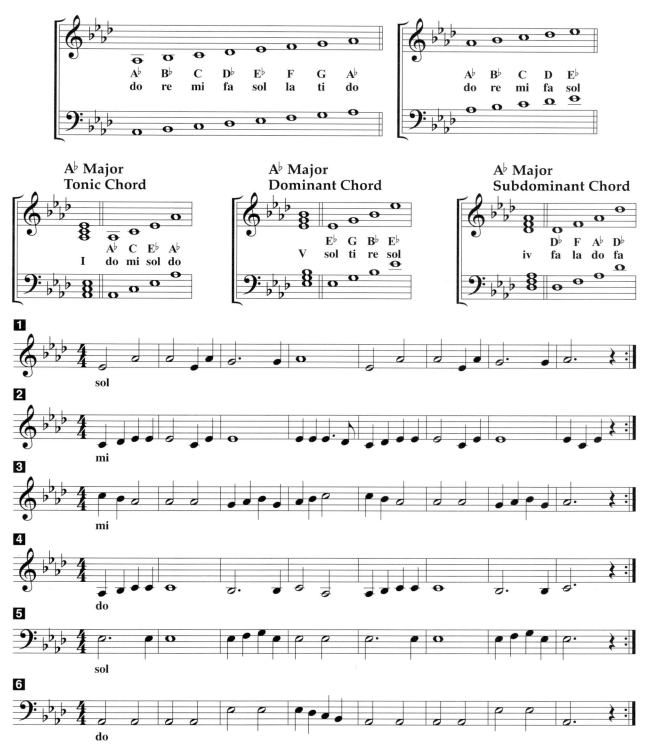

Practice

◆ Pitch and Rhythm • Key of F Minor

Using the F minor patterns below as a guide, sight-sing the following exercises separately or in any combination.

Practice

◆ Pitch and Rhythm • Key of E Major

Using the E major patterns below as a guide, sight-sing the following exercises separately or in any combination.

Practice

◆ Pitch and Rhythm • Key of C♯ Minor

Using the C♯ minor patterns below as a guide, sight-sing the following exercises separately or in any combination.

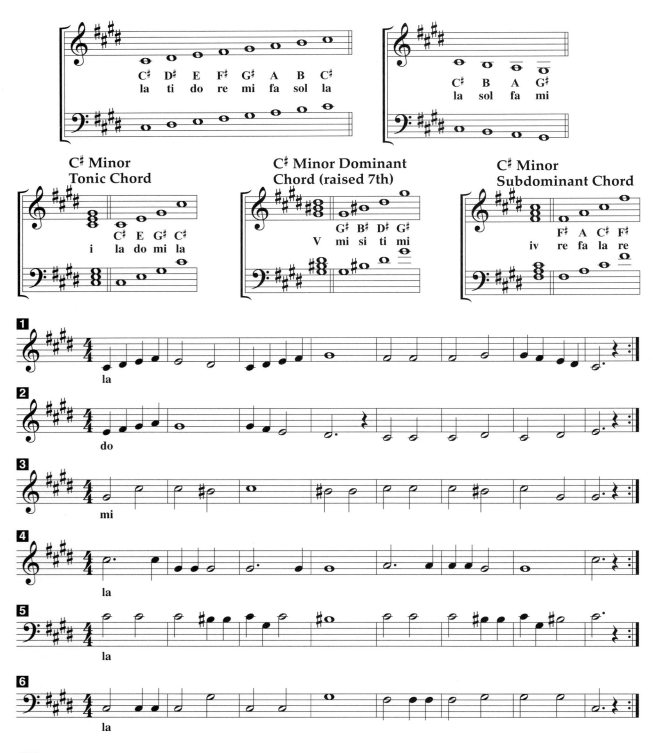

Pitch

◆ Modes and Modal Scales

Before major and minor keys and scales were developed, there was an earlier system of pitch organization called modes. Like major and minor scales, each modal scale is made up of a specific arrangement of whole steps and half steps, with the half steps occurring between *mi* and *fa,* and *ti* and *do.* Here are some examples of modal scales starting and ending on C.

Like the major scale, the **Ionian scale** is *a scale that starts and ends on* do.

∨ = half step

The **Dorian scale** is *a scale that starts and ends on* re.

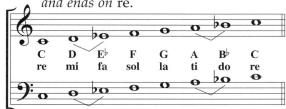

The **Phrygian scale** is *a scale that starts and ends on* mi.

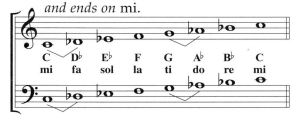

The **Lydian scale** is *a scale that starts and ends on* fa.

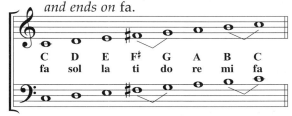

The **Mixolydian scale** is *a scale that starts and ends on* sol.

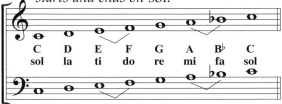

Like the minor scale, the **Aeolian scale** is *a scale that starts and ends on* la.

◆ Practice

Sight-sing the following exercise that uses pitches found in the C Dorian scale.

Practice

◆ Pitch and Rhythm • The D Dorian and F Lydian Scales

Sight-sing the following sets of exercises separately or in any combination.

◆ The D Dorian Scale

The D Dorian scale starts and ends on D, or *re*, and its half steps are between E and F (*mi* and *fa*) and B and C (*ti* and *do*). Sing the D Dorian scale and exercises.

◆ The F Lydian Scale

The F Lydian scale starts and ends on F, or *fa*, and its half steps are between B and C (*ti* and *do*) and E and F (*mi* and *fa*). Sing the F Lydian scale and exercises.

Practice

◆ Pitch • The D Mixolydian Scale

The D Mixolydian scale starts and ends on D, or *sol,* and its half steps are between F♯ and G *(ti* and *do)* and B and C *(mi* and *fa).* Notice the F♯ in the key signature. Sing the D Mixolydian scale before singing the following song.

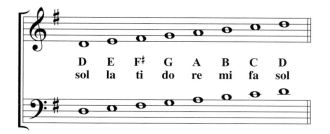

This Festive Night

Words and Music by
AUDREY SNYDER

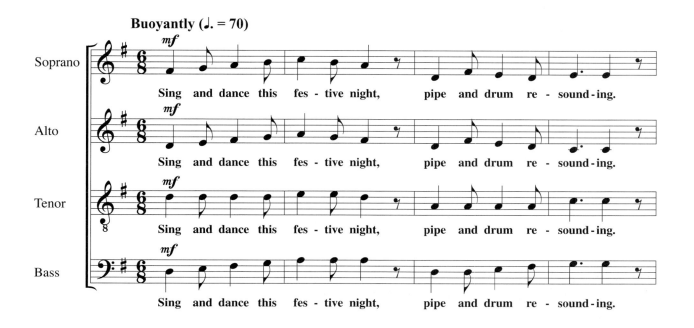

Happy hearts and spirits bright, love and joy abounding.

Happy hearts and spirits bright, love and joy abounding.

Happy hearts and spirits bright, love and joy abounding.

Happy hearts and spirits bright, love and joy abounding.

Fa la la la la la la la la, fa la la la la la.

Fa la la la la la, fa la la la la la la.

Fa la la la la la la la, fa la la la la la la.

Fa la la la la la la la, fa la la la la la.

Fa la la la la la la la la, sing with joy!

Fa la la la la la la la, sing with joy!

Fa la la la la la la la la, sing with joy!

Fa la la la la la, sing with joy!

Evaluation

Demonstrate what you have learned in Chapter Nine by completing the following:

◆ ## Sharps or Flats?
Using the keyboard below as a guide, answer the following questions.
1. The key signature of E major has four sharps or four flats?
2. The key signature of F minor has four sharps or four flats?

◆ Before major and minor scales developed, what kind of scales were used for organizing pitch?

◆ Sing the following melodies. What key are each in?

An Upscale Home On The Range

Sad Star

la

la

A♭ Harmonization

The Phrygian Pigeon

Step,   step,   neck thrust-ing out,   the Phry-gian pi - geon struts to his   nest on — high,
(mi)

Step,   step,   peck - ing a - bout,   Aren't you glad that   cows don't fly?

CHAPTER 10

Rhythm

◆ Borrowed Division • Triplets and Duplets

The **beat** is *the steady pulse of all music.*

Simple meter is *any meter in which the quarter note receives the beat, and the division of the beat is based on two eighth notes.* $\frac{2}{4}$, $\frac{3}{4}$ and $\frac{4}{4}$ meters are examples of simple meter.

Compound meter is *any meter in which the dotted quarter note receives the beat, and the division of the beat is based on three eighth notes.* $\frac{6}{8}$ is an example of compound meter.

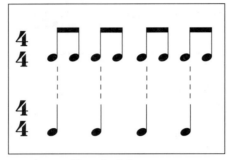
Simple Meter

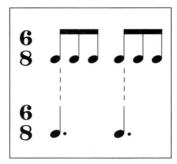
Compound Meter

Sometimes in simple meter, it is necessary for the beat to be divided into three. Likewise, in compound meter, it is sometimes necessary for the beat to be divided into two. When this happens, it is known as the borrowed division of the beat.

In simple meter, the borrowed division is called a triplet, since it is a division of three where two would normally be. In compound meter, the borrowed division is called a duplet, since it is a division of two where three would normally be.

Look at the following examples and notice how these are notated with a bracket over the borrowed grouping of notes. In some cases, there is only a number and no bracket.

◆ Practice

Clap, tap or chant while conducting the following exercises to practice reading triplets and duplets. Keep the beat steady.

Rhythm

◆ More About Triplets and Duplets

Any note value can be a triplet or duplet. Here are some other examples.

◆ Quarter Note Triplets

In simple meter, a quarter note triplet occupies the same amount of time as two quarter notes or one half note. Practice the following patterns until you can perform the quarter note triplet evenly.

◆ Half Note Triplets

In simple meter, a half note triplet occupies the same amount of time as two half notes or one whole note. Practice the following patterns until you can perform the half note triplet evenly.

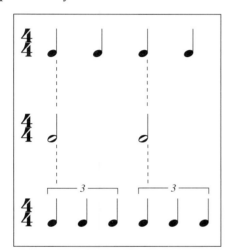

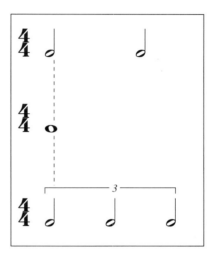

◆ Practice

Clap, tap or chant while conducting the following exercises to practice reading triplets and duplets. Keep the beat steady.

Rhythm

◆ More About Mixed Meter

A common practice, especially in contemporary music, is the use of **mixed meter**, or *a technique in which the time signature or meter changes frequently within a piece of music.*

Also found in contemporary music is **assymetric meter**, *a meter in which the strong beats create combinations of groups of two and three.*

$\frac{5}{4}$ can be grouped as: 2 + 3
3 + 2

$\frac{7}{4}$ can be grouped as: 3 + 4
4 + 3
2 + 2 + 3 (and other groupings)

$\frac{11}{4}$ can be grouped as: 4 + 4 + 3
2 + 2 + 3 + 2 + 2
3 + 3 + 3 + 2 (and other groupings)

Another common practice is to group eighth notes in unequal groups, such as $\frac{5}{8}$ or $\frac{7}{8}$. It is also possible to group eighth notes in unequal groups in more common meters such as $\frac{4}{4}$ or $\frac{6}{8}$ meter.

Unlike triplets and duplets, in these meters, the eighth note division remains constant, and the beat is made longer or shorter based on the number of eighth notes.

◆ Practice

Clap, tap or chant while conducting the following exercises, keeping the eighth note division constant.

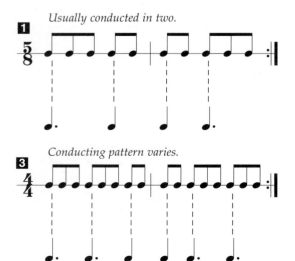

Usually conducted in two.

1

Usually conducted in three.

2

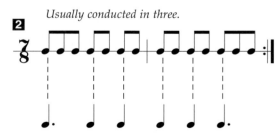

Conducting pattern varies.

3

Conducted in two or three.

4

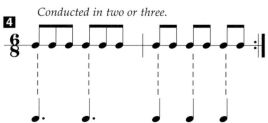

Practice

◆ Pitch and Rhythm • Mixed Meter • Asymetric Meter
Sight-sing the following unequal and mixed meter exercises in various keys.

Jubilate Deo

Psalm 100

Music by
EMILY CROCKER

Pitch

◆ The Blues Scale

The blues scale is a six-note scale that developed out of the songs and music of African Americans during and following the slavery era. In the blues scale, the second and sixth notes are often omitted, and the third, fifth and seventh notes are lowered (or flatted).

The blues became very popular in the early decades of the twentieth century and later formed the roots of jazz, country and rock and roll.

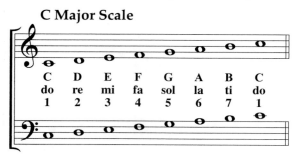

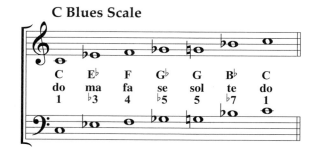

◆ Practice

Sight-sing the following exercises that use pitches found in the blues scale.

*G♭ (se) and F♯ (fi) are the same pitch and may be used interchangeably.

Rhythm

◆ Swing Rhythms

In many jazz, blues and pop styles of music, swing rhythms are often used. **Swing rhythms** are *rhythms in which the second eighth note of each beat is played or sung like the last third of a triplet.*

Dotted patterns are also common in swing rhythms and are played or sung like triplets.

◆ Practice

Sight-sing the following exercises separately or in any combination. The nonsense words are sometimes called "scat" syllables, and are often used by jazz singers.

Singin' the Blues

Words and Music by
EMILY CROCKER

Pitch

◆ Intervals

An **interval** is *the distance between two notes.* The basic intervals are seconds, thirds, fourths, fifths, sixths, sevenths and octaves. There are larger intervals, but they can be expressed as the combination of smaller intervals. (For example, a ninth is the combination of an octave plus a second.)

Here are some examples of basic diatonic intervals in the key of C major.

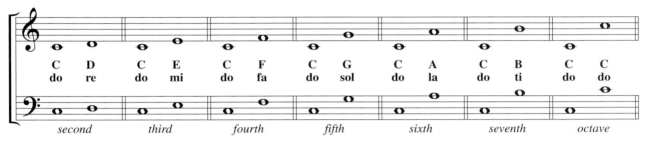

◆ Practice

Identify the intervals in the following examples.

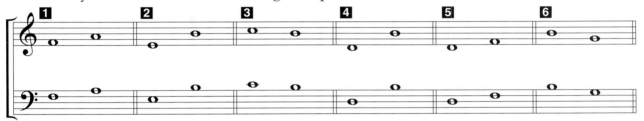

◆ Consonant and Dissonant Intervals

Intervals can be consonant or dissonant. Concepts of consonance and dissonance have changed over time, but in Western European music, consonance generally refers to intervals and chords that provide what can be described as normalcy or repose, while dissonant intervals and chords represent disturbance or tension.

Consonant intervals can be described as intervals of the major and minor triads: the third, fourth, fifth, sixth and octave. (Note: A fourth is an inverted fifth. A sixth is an inverted third.)

Dissonant intervals can be described as all other intervals: second, seventh, and diminished and augmented intervals.

◆ Practice

Sing the following chord patterns that use dissonant intervals. Listen to the harmonic tension produced by the dissonance. Notice that the tension resolves when each chord returns to consonance.

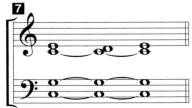 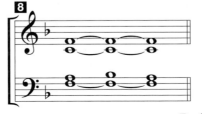 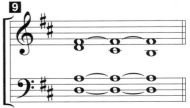

Prayer

Words and Music by
EMILY CROCKER

Evaluation

Demonstrate what you have learned in Chapter Ten by completing the following:

◆ Triplets and Duplets

1. In what kind of meters would triplets normally be used?
2. In what kind of meters would duplets normally be used?

◆ Be A Composer

1. Each of these rhythm patterns equals one beat in $\frac{3}{4}$ meter. Create a rhythm composition in $\frac{3}{4}$ meter with three beats per measure.

2. Each of these rhythm patterns equals one beat in $\frac{6}{8}$ meter. Create a rhythm composition in $\frac{6}{8}$ meter with two beats per measure.

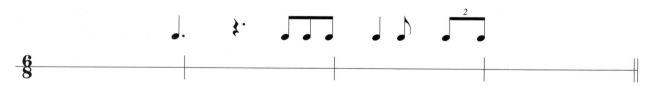

◆ Challenge

Using rhythmic patterns from Exercise 1 and Exercise 2 from above, create a four-measure composition in assymetric meter.

◆ Consonant and Dissonant Intervals

Identify the intervals below. Which intervals are consonant and which are dissonant?

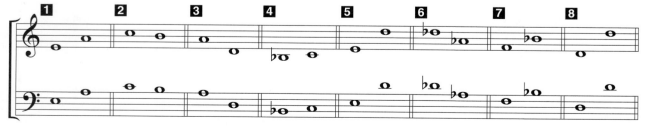

Appendix

To The Teacher 180

How To Use This Book 180

National Standards For Music Education – Grades 9–12 .181

Chapter Overviews • Focuses • Evaluation Answers 185

Pitch – Sight-Singing Method • Movable *Do* In Major Keys 190

Pitch – Sight-Singing Method • Movable *Do* In Minor Keys 191

Pitch – Sight-Singing Method • Fixed *Do* In Major Keys 192

Pitch – Sight-Singing Method • Fixed *Do* In Minor Keys 193

Pitch – Sight-Singing Method • Numbers In Major Keys .194

Pitch – Sight-Singing Method • Numbers In Minor Keys .195

Rhythm – Counting Methods • Simple Meter 196

Rhythm – Counting Methods • Compound Meter 198

Practice – Rhythm • Simple Meter 199

Practice – Rhythm • Dotted Notes 200

Practice – Rhythm • Compound Meter 201

Pitch – The Circle of Fifths 202

Pitch – The Piano Keyboard 203

To The Teacher

EXPERIENCING CHORAL MUSIC–Proficient Sight-Singing is designed to provide a sequential program to be used in the choral classroom for the study of music theory and music reading skills. For students to gain the most from this material, plan 10–15 minutes of daily study, including the introduction of new material, as well as the practice and review of previous material.

◆ Features of the Program
- The sequence is pedagogically sound and practical.
- The terminology is accurate and literal.
- Music theory is presented in a format that is compatible with the material in the *EXPERIENCING CHORAL MUSIC* repertoire books. Cross-references are provided in each repertoire book to the coordinating concepts in this book.
- It is designed to be successful within a variety of choral organizations: treble, tenor/bass or mixed.

How To Use This Book

EXPERIENCING CHORAL MUSIC–Proficient Sight-Singing is organized into 12 chapters that include material for developing skills in music theory, sight-singing melodic exercises, and sight-reading rhythmic exercises. Songs to sight-sing that cover the concepts introduced in each chapter are also included. Various musical terms and symbols are introduced. Finally, each chapter concludes with a comprehensive evaluation.

◆ Sight-Singing
The sight-singing exercises and songs are designed to allow students to practice the concepts presented in each chapter. Included in this material are:
- Various musical terms and symbols.
- The use of solfège syllables to identify and sing correct pitches.
- Echo-singing and group practice exercises.
- Combinable exercises that provide practice in unison sight-singing and part-singing.

◆ Methods of Sight-Singing
There are many good methods to use in developing sight-singing skills. For the melodic exercises, consider using numbers or solfège syllables (movable or fixed *do*). For rhythm reading, consider the Eastman, Traditional or Kodály methods. It is important to be consistent and use the same method daily. More information about each method is included in this Appendix.

National Standards High School Grades 9–12

The National Standards for Music Education were developed by the Music Educators National Conference. Reprinted by permission.

Music

The study of music contributes in important ways to the quality of every student's life. Every musical work is a product of its time and place, although some works transcend their original settings and continue to appeal to humans through their timeless and universal attraction. Through singing, playing instruments and composing, students can express themselves creatively, while a knowledge of notation and performance traditions enables them to learn new music independently throughout their lives. Skills in analysis, evaluation and synthesis are important because they enable students to recognize and pursue excellence in the musical experiences and to understand and enrich their environment. Because music is an integral part of human history, the ability to listen with understanding is essential if students are to gain a broad cultural and historical perspective. The adult life of every student is enriched by the skills, knowledge and habits acquired in the study of music.

Every course in music, including performance courses, should provide instruction in creating, performing, listening to and analyzing music, in addition to focusing on its specific subject matter.

1. **Content Standard:** Singing, alone and with others, a varied repertoire of music
   Achievement Standard, Proficient:
   Students
   a. sing with *expression and *technical accuracy a large and varied repertoire of vocal literature with a *level of difficulty of 4, on a scale of 1 to 6, including some songs performed from memory
   b. sing music written in four parts, with and without accompaniment
   c. demonstrate well-developed ensemble skills
   Achievement Standard, Advanced:
   Students
   d. sing with expression and technical accuracy a large and varied repertoire of vocal literature with a level of difficulty of 5, on a scale of 1 to 6
   e. sing music written in more than four parts
   f. sing in small ensembles with one student on a part

2. **Content Standard:** Performing on instruments, alone and with others, a varied repertoire of music
   Achievement Standard, Proficient:
   Students
   a. perform with expression and technical accuracy a large and varied repertoire of instrumental literature with a level of difficulty of 4, on a scale of 1 to 6
   b. perform an appropriate part in an ensemble, demonstrating well-developed

ensemble skills

    c. perform in small ensembles with one student on a part

Achievement Standard, Advanced:

Students

    d. perform with expression and technical accuracy a large and varied repertoire of instrumental literature with a level of difficulty of 5, on a scale of 1 to 6.

3. **Content Standard:** Improvising melodies, variations and accompaniments

    Achievement Standard, Proficient:

Students

    a. improvise stylistically appropriate harmonizing parts

    b. improvise rhythmic and melodic variations on given pentatonic melodies and melodies in major and minor keys

    c. improvise original melodies over given chord progressions, each in a consistent *style, *meter and *tonality

    Achievement Standard, Advanced:

Students

    d. improvise stylistically appropriate harmonizing parts in a variety of styles

    e. improvise original melodies in a variety of styles, over given chord progressions, each in a consistent style, meter and tonality

4. **Content Standard:** Composing and arranging music within specified guidelines

    Achievement Standard, Proficient:

Students

    a. compose music in several distinct styles, demonstrating creativity in using the *elements of music for expressive effect

    b. arrange pieces for voices or instruments other than those for which the pieces were written in ways that preserve or enhance the expressive effect of the music

    c. compose and arrange music for voices and various acoustic and electronic instruments, demonstrating knowledge of the ranges and traditional usages of the sound sources

    Achievement Standard, Advanced:

Students

    d. compose music, demonstrating imagination and technical skill in applying the principles of composition

5. **Content Standard:** Reading and notating music

    Achievement Standard, Proficient:

Students

    a. demonstrate the ability to read an instrumental or vocal score of up to four *staves by describing how the elements of music are used

Students who participate in a choral or instrumental ensemble or class

    b. sight-read, accurately and expressively, music with a level of difficulty of 3, on a scale of 1 to 6

Achievement Standard, Advanced:

Students

    c. demonstrate the ability to read a full instrumental or vocal score by describing how the elements of music are used and explaining all transpositions and clefs

    d. interpret nonstandard notation symbols used by some 20th century [sic] composers

Students who participate in a choral or instrumental ensemble or class

    e. sight-read, accurately and expressively, music with a level of difficulty of 4, on a scale of 1 to 6

6. **Content Standard:** Listening to, analyzing and describing music

    Achievement Standard, Proficient:

Students

    a. analyze aural examples of a varied repertoire of music, representing diverse *genres and cultures, by describing the uses of elements of music and expressive devices

    b. demonstrate extensive knowledge of the technical vocabulary of music

    c. identify and explain compositional devices and techniques used to provide unity and variety and tension and release in a musical work and give examples of other works that make similar uses of these devices and techniques

    Achievement Standard, Advanced:

Students

    d. demonstrate the ability to perceive and remember music events by describing in detail significant events[1] occurring in a given aural example

    e. compare ways in which musical materials are used in a given example relative to ways they are used in other works of the same genre or style

    f. analyze and describe uses of the elements of music in a given work that make it unique, interesting and expressive

7. **Content Standard:** Evaluating music and music performances

    Achievement Standard, Proficient:

Students

    a. evolve specific criteria for making informed, critical evaluations of the quality and effectiveness of performances, compositions, arrangements and improvisations and apply the criteria in their personal participation in music

    b. evaluate a performance, composition, arrangement or improvisation by comparing it to similar or exemplary models

    Achievement Standard, Advanced:

Students

    c. evaluate a given musical work in terms of its aesthetic qualities and explaining the musical means is uses to evoke feelings and emotions

8. **Content Standard:** Understanding relationships between music, the other arts, and disciplines outside the arts

    Achievement Standard, Proficient:

Students

a. explain how elements, artistic processes (such as imagination or craftsmanship), and organizational principles (such as unity and variety or repetition and contrast) are used in similar and distinctive ways in the various arts and cite examples

b. compare characteristics of two or more arts within a particular historical period or style and cite examples from various cultures

c. explain ways in which the principles and subject matter of various disciplines outside the arts are interrelated with those of music[2]

Achievement Standard, Advanced:

Students

d. compare the uses of characteristic elements, artistic processes and organizational principles among the arts in different historical periods and different cultures

e. explain how the roles of creators, performers, and others involved in the production and presentation of the arts are similar to and different from one another in the various arts[3]

9. **Content Standard:** Understanding music in relation to history and culture

Achievement Standard, Proficient:

Students

a. classify by genre or style and by historical period or culture unfamiliar but representative aural examples of music and explain the reasoning behind their classifications

b. identify sources of American music genres,[4] trace the evolution of those genres, and cite well-known musicians associated with them

c. identify various roles[5] that musicians perform, cite representative individuals who have functioned in each role, and describe their activities and achievements

Achievement Standard, Advanced:

Students

d. identify and explain the stylistic features of a given musical work that serve to define its aesthetic tradition and its historical or cultural context

e. identify and describe music genres or styles that show the influence of two or more cultural traditions, identify the cultural source of each influence, and trace the historical conditions that produced the synthesis of influences

Terms identified by an asterisk (*) are explained further in the glossary of National Standards for Arts Education, published by Music Educators National Conference, © 1994.

1. E.g., fugal entrances, chromatic modulations, developmental devices

2. E.g., language arts: compare the ability of music and literature to convey images, feeling and meanings; physics: describe the physical basis of tone production in string, wind, percussion and electronic instruments and the human voice and of the transmission and perception of sound

3. E.g., creators: painters, composers, choreographers, playwrights; performers: instrumentalists, singers, dancers, actors; others: conductors, costumers, directors, lighting designers

4. E.g., swing, Broadway musical, blues

5. E.g., entertainer, teacher, transmitter of cultural tradition

CHAPTER OVERVIEWS • FOCUSES • EVALUATION ANSWERS

Book Overview

Throughout this book, concepts in pitch and rhythm, along with definitions of music terminology, are presented. Exercises to practice are included for each concept. These exercises are in the form of echo singing, drills and combinable lines (lines that may be sung individually or in any combination). Sight-singing songs are provided that place the new concepts in the context of a song. By sight-singing the song successfully, students demonstrate mastery of the new concept. The evaluation section at the end of each chapter assesses the concepts presented in the chapter.

Chapter One Overview

In Chapter One, the staff, treble and bass clefs, grand staff, barline and measure are introduced. Beat, quarter note and rest, half note and rest, dotted half note, and whole note and rest are presented, along with 4/4 meter. The C major scale is presented.

Chapter One Focus
- Demonstrate well-developed ensemble skills. *(NS 1c)*
- Sight-read, accurately and expressively, music with a level difficulty of 3, on a scale of 1 to 6. *(NS 5b)*

Chapter One Evaluation
Answers to Questions on page 12:
- *First Bullet: Name the Notes*
  The first five notes of the C major scale are: C, D, E, F, G, or *do, re, mi, fa, sol.*
- *Second Bullet: 4/4 Meter*
  The top number means there are four beats in a measure and the bottom number means that the quarter note receives the beat.
- *Third Bullet: Name the Kind of Notes*
  From left to right: **(a)** half note; **(b)** whole note; **(c)** quarter note; **(d)** dotted half note;

(e) quarter rest; **(f)** whole rest; **(g)** half rest.
- *Fourth Bullet: Mental Musical Math*
  (1) two quarter notes are equal to the same amount of time as one half note; **(2)** a dotted half note equals the same amount of time as three quarter notes.
- *Fifth Bullet: Sight-Singing Exercises*
  Check for accurate pitch and rhythm while maintaining a steady beat.

Chapter Two Overview

In Chapter Two, 3/4 meter is introduced, as well as the C major and A minor scales. Practice exercises and sight-singing songs are provided in 3/4 meter for both keys. Ledger lines are defined and used within practice exercises and the sight-singing song.

Chapter Two Focus
- Demonstrate well-developed ensemble skills. *(NS 1c)*
- Compose music demonstrating creativity in using the elements of music. *(NS 4a)*
- Sight-read, accurately and expressively, music with a level difficulty of 3, on a scale of 1 to 6. *(NS 5b)*
- Demonstrate extensive knowledge of the technical vocabulary of music. *(NS 6b)*

Chapter Two Evaluation
Answers to Questions on page 22:
- *First Bullet: Name the Notes*
  The notes in the C major scale are: C, D, E, F, G, A, B, C or *do, re, mi, fa, sol, la, ti, do.* The half steps occur between E and F (*mi* and *fa*) and between B and C (*ti* and *do*). The notes in the A minor scale are: A, B, C, D, E, F, G, A or *la, ti, do, re, mi, fa, sol, la.* The half steps occur between B and C (*ti* and *do*) and between E and F (*mi* and *fa*).

- *Second Bullet: Sight-Singing Melodies*
Check for accurate pitch and rhythm while maintaining a steady beat.
- *Third Bullet: Be A Composer*
Each composition will be different. Check for correct rhythms. Provide students the opportunity to play their compositions on rhythm instruments. Additional opportunity to add pitches and transfer to a staff will require a review for accuracy of key choice, notes and rhythm patterns. Review/discuss lyric choices.

Chapter Three Overview

In Chapter Three, eighth notes and rests, as well as grouped eighth notes, are presented. The double bar and repeat sign are defined. Altered pitches and accidentals are presented. The altered pitch names in solfège syllables are also introduced. Tonic and dominant chords are presented in the keys of C major and A minor, followed by combinable practice lines and a sight-singing song. The natural, harmonic and melodic minor scales are defined. Tied notes are explained.

Chapter Three Focus
- Demonstrate well-developed ensemble skills. *(NS 1c)*
- Sight-read, accurately and expressively, music with a level difficulty of 3, on a scale of 1 to 6. *(NS 5b)*
- Demonstrate extensive knowledge of the technical vocabulary of music. *(NS 6b)*

Chapter Three Evaluation
Answers to Questions on page 43:
- *First Bullet: Major Tonic*
(1) *do, mi, sol;* (2) C, E, G.
- *Second Bullet: Minor Tonic*
(1) *la, do, mi;* (2) A, C, E.
- *Third Bullet: Name the Kind of Notes and Rests*
From left to right: (a) eighth note; (b) eighth rest; (c) two eighth notes grouped together.
- *Fourth Bullet: Musical Math*
When the quarter note receives the beat: (1) true; (2) true; (3) false; (4) false; (5) true; (6) true.

- *Fifth Bullet: Sight-Singing Exercises*
Check for accurate pitch and rhythm while maintaining a steady beat.

Chapter Three Evaluation
Answers to Questions on page 44:
- *First Bullet: The Three Minor Scales*
(1) A, B, C, D, E, F, G, A and *la, ti, do, re, mi, fa, sol, la;* (2) *fa* becomes *fi* and *sol* becomes *si;* (3) G♯.
- *Second Bullet: True or False?*
(1) false – the dominant chord is built on the fifth note of the scale; (2) true.
- *Third Bullet: Answer the Questions*
(1) *sol, ti, re;* (2) G, B, D; (3) *mi, sol, ti;* (4) *mi, si, ti.*
- *Fourth Bullet: Sight-Singing Exercises*
Check for accuracy of pitch and rhythm while maintaining a steady beat.

Chapter Four Overview

In Chapter Four, the F major and D minor scales, along with tonic and dominant chords, are introduced. Tied notes are reviewed. Dotted half and quarter notes are presented. Dynamics are introduced. Sight-singing songs in F major and D minor are featured.

Chapter Four Focus
- Sing music written in four parts, with and without accompaniment. *(NS 1b)*
- Demonstrate well-developed ensemble skills. *(NS 1c)*
- Demonstrate the ability to read a vocal score of up to four staves by describing how the elements of music are used. *(NS 5a)*
- Sight-read, accurately and expressively, music with a level difficulty of 3, on a scale of 1 to 6. *(NS 5b)*
- Demonstrate extensive knowledge of the technical vocabulary of music. *(NS 6b)*

Chapter Four Evaluation
Answers to Questions on page 61:
- *First Bullet: Musical Math*
When the quarter note receives the beat: (a) one half note plus one quarter note equals three beats; (b) one dotted half note plus one quarter note equals four beats; (c) one

quarter note plus one eighth note equals one and a half beats; **(d)** one dotted half note equals three beats; **(e)** one dotted quarter note equals one and a half beats; **(f)** one dotted quarter note plus one eighth note equals two beats.

- *Second Bullet: Rhythm Exercises*
  Check for accurate rhythm while maintaining a steady beat.
- *Third Bullet: Sight-Singing Melody*
  Check for accurate pitch and rhythm while maintaining a steady beat.

Chapter Five Overview

In Chapter Five, sixteenth notes and sixteenth and eighth note combinations are presented, followed by a speech chorus. 2/4 meter is defined, and combinable practice lines in the key of D minor are provided. The G major scale and E minor scale, along with the subdominant chord are introduced. Dotted eighth and sixteenth note combinations are introduced. Three sight-singing songs are provided.

Chapter Five Focus

- Sing music written in four parts, with and without accompaniment. *(NS 1b)*
- Demonstrate well-developed ensemble skills. *(NS 1c)*
- Demonstrate the ability to read a vocal score of up to four staves by describing how the elements of music are used. *(NS 5a)*
- Sight-read, accurately and expressively, music with a level difficulty of 3, on a scale of 1 to 6. *(NS 5b)*
- Demonstrate extensive knowledge of the technical vocabulary of music. *(NS 6b)*

Chapter Five Evaluation

Answers to Questions on page 84:

- *First Bullet: Musical Math*
  When the quarter note receives the beat:
  (1) yes; **(2)** yes; **(3)** no, a dotted eighth and sixteenth note combination would equal one quarter note; **(4)** yes.

- *Second Bullet: 2/4 Meter*
  There are two beats per measure and the quarter note receives the beat.
- *Third Bullet: Rhythm Exercise*
  Check for accurate rhythm while maintaining a steady beat.
- *Fourth Bullet: Answer the Questions*
  (1) Fifth note, *sol;* **(2)** Fourth note, *fa;* **(3)** Fifth note, *mi;* **(4)** Fourth note, *re.*
- *Fifth Bullet: Sight-Singing Exercises*
  Exercise 1 is in E minor; exercise 2 is in G major. Check for accurate pitch and rhythm while maintaining a steady beat.

Chapter Six Overview

In Chapter Six, syncopation and mixed meter, along with the symbol for accent, are introduced. Practice lines in syncopation are given in the key of E minor. The B♭ major and G minor scales, along with their corresponding tonic, dominant and subdominant chords, are presented in exercises and combinable lines. Diatonic chords are explained. Three sight-singing songs and a rhythmic speech chorus reinforce all concepts.

Chapter Six Focus

- Sing music written in four parts, with and without accompaniment. *(NS 1b)*
- Demonstrate well-developed ensemble skills. *(NS 1c)*
- Compose music demonstrating creativity in using the elements of music. *(NS 4a)*
- Demonstrate the ability to read a vocal score of up to four staves by describing how the elements of music are used. *(NS 5a)*
- Sight-read, accurately and expressively, music with a level difficulty of 3, on a scale of 1 to 6. *(NS 5b)*
- Demonstrate extensive knowledge of the technical vocabulary of music. *(NS 6b)*

Chapter Six Evaluation

Answers to Questions on page 112:

- *First Bullet: Be A Composer*
  Each composition will be different. Check for correct rhythm and pitch. Provide students

the opportunity to play their compositions.
- *Second Bullet: Primary and Diatonic Chords*
  (1) Tonic, I; **(2)** Subdominant, IV; **(3)** Dominant, V; **(4)** Tonic, I; **(5)** Mediant, iii; **(6)** Submediant, vi **(7)** Supertonic, ii; **(8)** Leading tone, vii°.

Chapter Seven Overview

In Chapter Seven, simple meter and compound meter are introduced. Tonic, dominant and subdominant chords in the key of E♭ major and C minor are presented. Division of the beat, mixed meters and combinations of meters are explained. Sight-singing songs and a rhythmic speech chorus are provided.

Chapter Seven Focus
- Sing music written in four parts, with and without accompaniment. *(NS 1b)*
- Demonstrate well-developed ensemble skills. *(NS 1c)*
- Demonstrate the ability to read a vocal score of up to four staves by describing how the elements of music are used. *(NS 5a)*
- Sight-read, accurately and expressively, music with a level difficulty of 3, on a scale of 1 to 6. *(NS 5b)*
- Demonstrate extensive knowledge of the technical vocabulary of music. *(NS 6b)*

Chapter Seven Evaluation
Answers to Questions on page 136:
- *First Bullet: True or False?*
  (1) false, simple meter **(2)** true; **(3)** true; **(4)** true
- *Second Bullet: Rhythm Exercises*
  Check for accurate rhythm while maintaining a steady beat.
- *Third Bullet: E♭ Major or C Minor?*
  (1) E♭ major; I, IV, V, I; **(2)** C minor; i, iv, v, i; **(3)** C minor; i, V, iv, i.
- *Fourth Bullet: Sight-Singing Exercise*
  Check for accurate pitch, rhythm, and conducting patterns while maintaining a steady beat.

Chapter Seven Evaluation
Answers to Questions on page 137:

- *First Bullet: Sight-Singing Exercises*
  Exercise 1 is in C minor and exercise 2 is in E♭ major. Check for accurate pitch and rhythm while maintaining a steady beat.
- *Second Bullet: Challenge*
  Check for accurate conducting patterns.

Chapter Eight Overview

In Chapter Eight, the keys of A major and F♯ minor are introduced with practice examples and a sight-singing song. Additional explanation of simple meter is included, along with 2/2 meter and cut time.

Chapter Eight Focus
- Sing music written in four parts, with and without accompaniment. *(NS 1b)*
- Demonstrate well-developed ensemble skills. *(NS 1c)*
- Compose music demonstrating creativity in using the elements of music. *(NS 4a)*
- Demonstrate the ability to read a vocal score of up to four staves by describing how the elements of music are used. *(NS 5a)*
- Sight-read, accurately and expressively, music with a level difficulty of 3, on a scale of 1 to 6. *(NS 5b)*
- Demonstrate extensive knowledge of the technical vocabulary of music. *(NS 6b)*

Chapter Eight Evaluation
Answers to Questions on page 151:
- *First Bullet: Simple Meters*
  Each composition will be different. Check for correct rhythms. Provide students the opportunity to play their compositions on rhythm instruments. Additional opportunity to add pitches and transfer to a staff will require a review for accuracy of key choice, notes and rhythm patterns.
- *Second Bullet: Challenge*
  Each composition will be different. Check for accurate rhythm patterns in each meter and the correct number of beats.

Chapter Nine Overview

In Chapter Nine, the Circle of Fifths is

introduced. The scale, tonic chord, dominant chord and subdominant chord are presented in the following keys: A♭ major, F minor, E major and C♯ minor. Practice drills and combinable lines are given for each key. Modal scales are presented along with a sight-singing song.

Chapter Nine Focus
- Sing music written in four parts, with and without accompaniment. *(NS 1b)*
- Demonstrate well-developed ensemble skills. *(NS 1c)*
- Demonstrate the ability to read a vocal score of up to four staves by describing how the elements of music are used. *(NS 5a)*
- Sight-read, accurately and expressively, music with a level difficulty of 3, on a scale of 1 to 6. *(NS 5b)*
- Demonstrate extensive knowledge of the technical vocabulary of music. *(NS 6b)*

Chapter Nine Evaluation
Answers to Questions on page 162:
- *First Bullet: Sharps or Flats?*
  (1) sharps; **(2)** flats.
- *Second Bullet: Answer the Question*
  Pitch was organized into modes or modal scales.
- *Third Bullet: Sight-Singing Melodies (continues on page 163)*
  "An Upscale Home on the Range" is in E major. "Sad Star" is in C♯ minor. "A♭ Harmonization" is in A♭ major. "The Phrygian Pigeon" is in E Phrygian mode. Check for accurate pitch and rhythm while maintaining a steady beat.

Chapter Ten Overview
In Chapter Ten, borrowed division is defined with examples of duplets and triplets. Additional examples of simple meter are presented. The blues scale and swing rhythms are introduced. Consonant and dissonant intervals are presented. Three sight-singing songs are included for concept reinforcement.

Chapter Ten Focus
- Sing music written in four parts, with and without accompaniment. *(NS 1b)*
- Demonstrate well-developed ensemble skills. *(NS 1c)*
- Compose music demonstrating creativity in using the elements of music. *(NS 4a)*
- Demonstrate the ability to read a vocal score of up to four staves by describing how the elements of music are used. *(NS 5a)*
- Sight-read, accurately and expressively, music with a level difficulty of 3, on a scale of 1 to 6. *(NS 5b)*
- Demonstrate extensive knowledge of the technical vocabulary of music. *(NS 6b)*

Chapter Ten Evaluation
Answers to Questions on page 178:
- *First Bullet: Triplet and Duplet Review*
  (1) simple; **(2)** compound
- *Second Bullet: Be A Composer*
  Each composition will be different. Check for correct rhythm patterns in both exercises.
- *Third Bullet: Challenge*
  Provide students the opportunity to play their compositions on rhythm instruments. The opportunity to add pitches and transfer to a staff will require a review for accurate key choices, notes and rhythm patterns.
- *Fourth Bullet: Consonant and Dissonant Intervals*
  (1) 4th, consonant; **(2)** 2nd, dissonant; **(3)** 5th, consonant; **(4)** 2nd, dissonant; **(5)** 7th, dissonant; **(6)** 4th, consonant; **(7)** 4th, consonant; **(8)** octave, consonant.

Pitch

◆ **Sight-Singing Method • Movable Do in Major Keys**

Regardless of the key, *do* is always the first pitch of the scale.

◆ **Diatonic Scales**

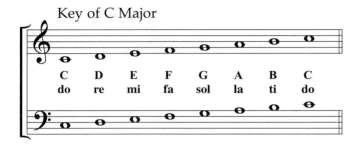

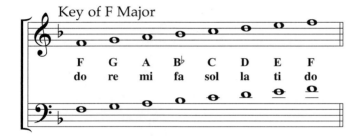

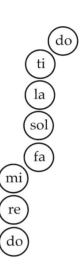

◆ **Chromatic Scales**

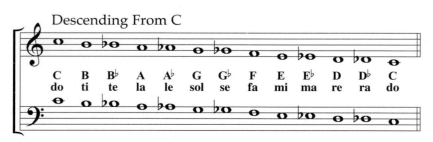

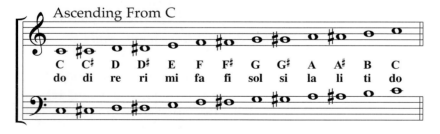

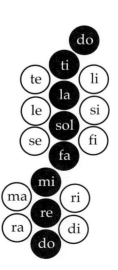

Pitch

◆ **Sight-Singing Method • Movable Do in Minor Keys**
Regardless of the key, *la* is always the first pitch of the scale.

◆ **The Natural Minor Scale**

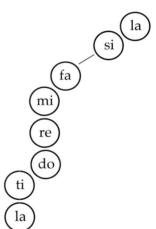

◆ **The Harmonic Minor Scale**

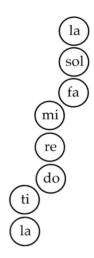

◆ **The Melodic Minor Scale**

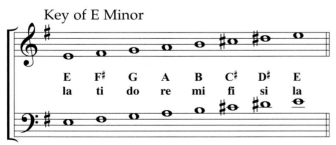

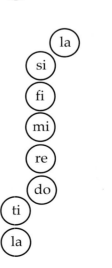

Pitch

◆ **Sight-Singing Method • Fixed Do in Major Keys**

Regardless of the key, *do* is always C.

◆ **Diatonic Scales**

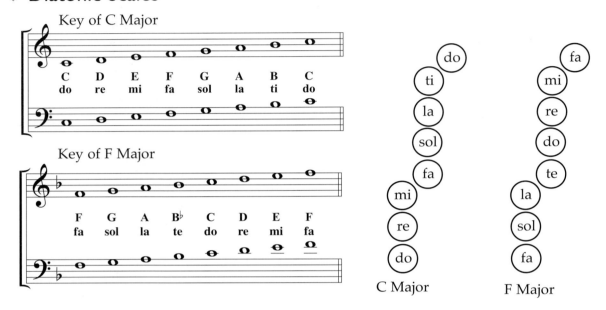

Key of C Major

C	D	E	F	G	A	B	C
do	re	mi	fa	sol	la	ti	do

Key of F Major

F	G	A	B♭	C	D	E	F
fa	sol	la	te	do	re	mi	fa

C Major   F Major

◆ **Chromatic Scales**

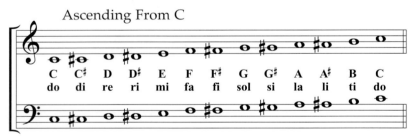

Ascending From C

C	C♯	D	D♯	E	F	F♯	G	G♯	A	A♯	B	C
do	di	re	ri	mi	fa	fi	sol	si	la	li	ti	do

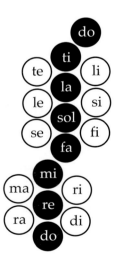

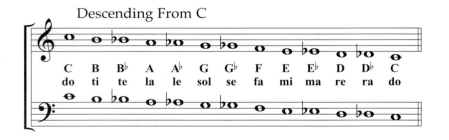

Descending From C

C	B	B♭	A	A♭	G	G♭	F	E	E♭	D	D♭	C
do	ti	te	la	le	sol	se	fa	mi	ma	re	ra	do

Pitch

◆ **Sight-Singing Method • Fixed Do in Minor Keys**
Regardless of the key, *la* is always A.

◆ **The Natural Minor Scale**

Key of A Minor

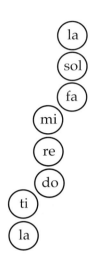

◆ **The Harmonic Minor Scale**

Key of D Minor

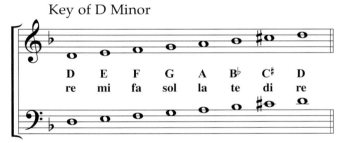

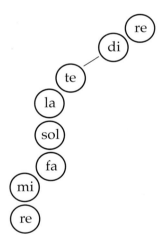

◆ **The Melodic Minor Scale**

Key of E Minor

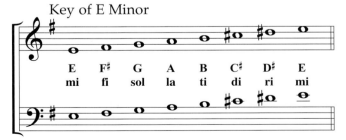

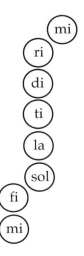

Pitch

◆ **Sight-Singing Method • Numbers in Major Keys**

Regardless of the key, "1" is always the first pitch of the scale.

◆ **Diatonic Scales**

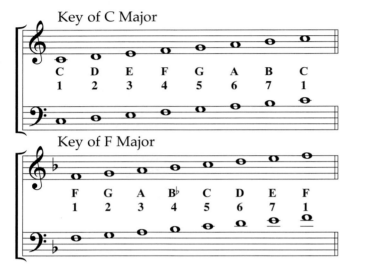

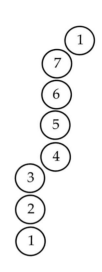

Accidentals can be performed either by singing the number but raising or lowering the pitch by a half step, or by singing the word "sharp" or "flat" before the number as a grace note.

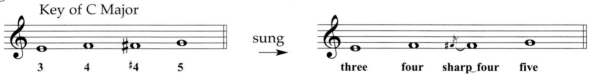

◆ **Chromatic Scales**

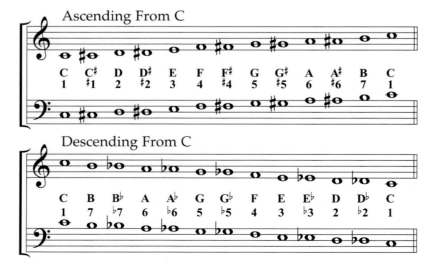

Pitch

◆ **Sight-Singing Method • Numbers in Minor Keys**

Regardless of the key, "6" is always the first pitch of the scale.

◆ **The Natural Minor Scale**

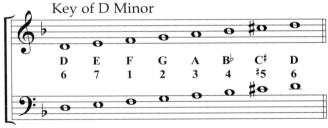

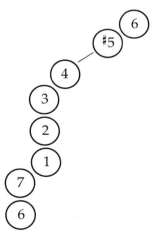

◆ **The Harmonic Minor Scale**

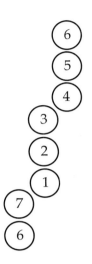

◆ **The Melodic Minor Scale**

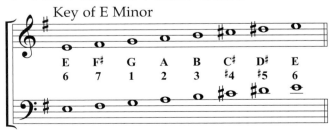

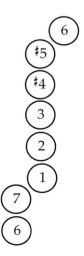

Rhythm

◆ Counting Methods • Simple Meter

Following are three methods in use for counting rhythms in simple meter.

Kodály	Traditional	Eastman
(Beat) 4/4 — ta ta ta ta	(Beat) 4/4 — 1 2 3 4	(Beat) 4/4 — 1 2 3 4
(Beat) 4/4 — ta - a ta - a	(Beat) 4/4 — 1____ 3____	(Beat) 4/4 — 1____ 3____
(Beat) 4/4 — ta - a - a - a	(Beat) 4/4 — 1_____	(Beat) 4/4 — 1_____
(Beat) 4/4 — ti ti ti ti ti ti ti ti	(Beat) 4/4 — 1 & 2 & 3 & 4 &	(Beat) 4/4 — 1 te 2 te 3 te 4 te
(Beat) 4/4 — ti ka ti ka ti ka ti ka ti ka ti ka ti ka ti ka	(Beat) 4/4 — 1 e & a 2 e & a 3 e & a 4 e & a	(Beat) 4/4 — 1 ta te ta 2 ta te ta 3 ta te ta 4 ta te ta
(Beat) 4/4 — ti ti ka ti ti ka ti ti ka ti ti ka	(Beat) 4/4 — 1 & a 2 & a 3 & a 4 & a	(Beat) 4/4 — 1 te ta 2 te ta 3 te ta 4 te ta

Rhythm

◆ Counting Methods • Simple Meter

Kodály	Traditional	Eastman

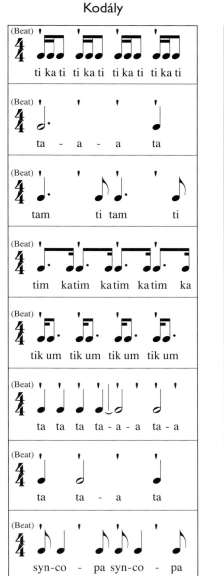

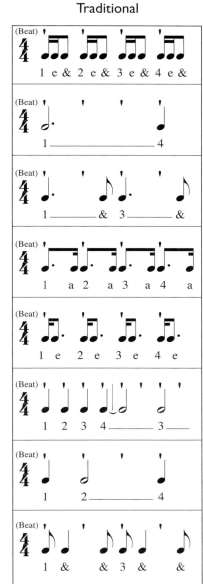

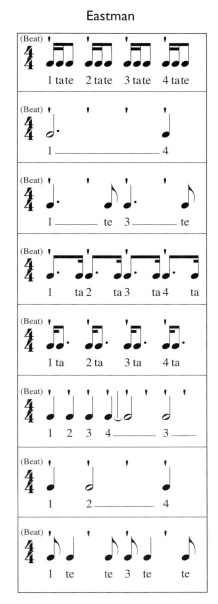

Rhythm

◆ Counting Methods • Compound Meter

Following are three methods in use for counting rhythms in compound meter.

Kodály	Traditional	Eastman
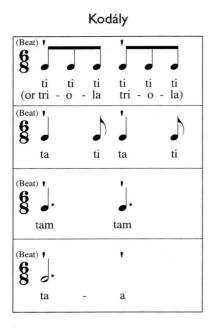	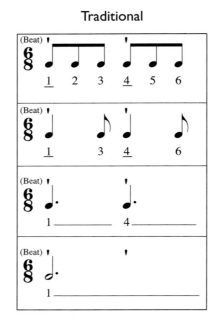	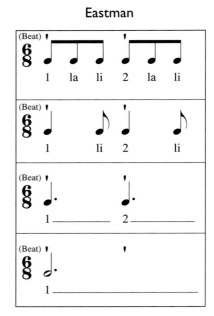

Practice

◆ Rhythm • Simple Meter

Clap, tap, or chant while conducting the following exercises.

Exercises Based on the Beat

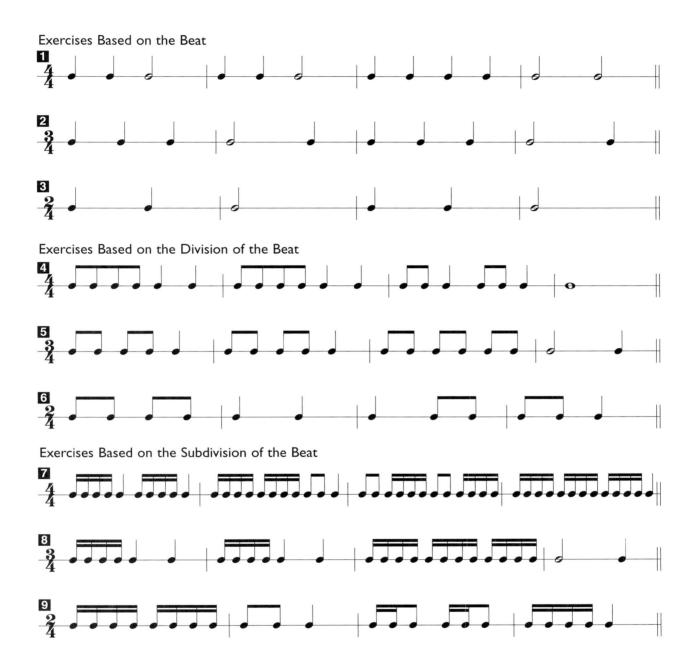

Exercises Based on the Division of the Beat

Exercises Based on the Subdivision of the Beat

Pitch

▲ The Circle of Fifths